Lost in Media

Lost in Media

**Migrant Perspectives
and the Public Sphere**

Edited by Ismail Einashe
and Thomas Roueché

With contributions by

Tania Bruguera
Moha Gerehou
Aleksandar Hemon
Lubaina Himid
Dawid Krawczyk
Antonija Letinić
Nesrine Malik
Nadifa Mohamed
Ece Temelkuran
Daniel Trilling
Menno Weijs
André Wilkens

Valiz, Amsterdam

CONTENTS

Contents

We Are Lost in Media

— André Wilkens

We are lost in media.

The media of the past have lost their business model. And the media of today seem only concerned with regaining a business model, no matter what. What stays behind is purpose, the purpose of media to create a functioning public space.

The digital world could be an ideal place for an enlightened public space, in principle. Instead it risks becoming an anti-enlightenment echo chamber where fact and fiction merge into some kind of post-factual universe, which produces post-factual winners such as Trump, Brexit and Orbán. Creating a functioning public sphere is of little interest to the click economy. Meanwhile, it destroys the economic foundations for quality journalism and calls it creative disruption. The resulting void is becoming a systemic risk to open societies, and to democracy as we know it.

This situation is even more acute at the European level because we are still imprisoned in national filter bubbles. The painful consequence is a vicious circle in which a lack of understanding of the 'other' leads to a lack of trust, which again leads to more stereotyping in the own echo chamber. We are lost in media.

But some are even more lost in media.

The migrant's journey is a physical and legal quest, but it is also a journey into another culture where the idea of 'them' meets the idea

André Wilkens

9

of 'us'. It's here that migrants enter into the rules of the news grid and a game of political power play based on exploiting popular prejudices. Migrants are constantly used in media to play the role of the stranger or the threat. And even if newspapers don't actively set out to vilify migrants, the sympathetic portrayal of the desperate victim in a boat is just as stigmatizing—as if people can only be seen through the lens of their trauma. The migrant as a multifaceted person with hopes and fears, family, friends, stories, a favourite football team and annoying habits is lost in media.

Against this backdrop, there's a young generation of migrants who are pushing the glass ceiling to enter the public sphere in Europe. By speaking up, they are diversifying the content that is spread through newspapers, TV channels, radio, websites or social media. They are complementing and challenging the stories that mainstream media are portraying on a daily basis.

A society can only be truly democratic if there is a public sphere in which different perspectives are shared and to which everyone has equal access. In the long term, European democracy will only work if it is underpinned by a European public sphere, rather than a series of fragmented national public spheres. Such a European public sphere needs media with a European purpose in which its actors and consumers do not feel lost. And this European public sphere must include the perspective of European migrants who will be part of shaping it.

Lost in Media is a reflection on the above themes of media, public space, migration and their disruptive and productive interaction. It gathers critical responses to the representations of migrants in the media in Europe through nine essays by prominent writers, artists, and journalists. The often personal reflections provide a perspective on Europe. A perspective in which migrants are the narrators, legitimate voices on the past, present, and future of Europe. Being lost in media is not a situation we can afford to tolerate.

The Power of the Story

— Ismail Einashe and Thomas Roueché

In July 2015, during a televised forum for young people, the German Chancellor Angela Merkel had an emotional encounter with Reem Sahwil, a young Palestinian refugee. Sahwil, whose family had arrived in the German city of Rostock from a refugee camp in Lebanon, told Merkel that they had been waiting for four years to gain permanent residency. 'It's really very hard to watch how other people can enjoy life and you yourself can't,' Sahwil told Merkel. 'I don't know what my future will bring.' The German Chancellor was blunt. Not all migrants could stay in Germany, she told the young girl, 'some will have to go home'. At these words, Sahwil began to cry. Merkel was speechless. She began to stroke the young girl's shoulder. Faced with such emotion Merkel stumbled, unable to explain her policies. Germany could not help every migrant, she told Sahwil. 'Politics is sometimes hard. You're right in front of me now and you're an extremely nice person. But you also know that in the Palestinian refugee camps in Lebanon there are thousands and thousands and if we were to say you can all come... we just can't manage it.'

What the media had begun to call the 'migrant crisis' played out on rolling news day after day over the summer and autumn of 2015 as over a million people made their way to Europe. The reality, of course, was more complicated: the vast majority of Syrians fleeing their nation's civil war stayed in Lebanon or Turkey; 80% of all migration in Africa is intra-African;

yet according to the news media, the 'migrant crisis' was of apocalyptic proportions. According to the media, 'hordes', 'floods' and 'waves' massed at the borders, putting the very existence of Europe at risk.

Merkel's meeting with Sahwil was a viral sensation across European media, a meeting that was symbolic of Europe's inhuman refusal to respond to the scale of this humanitarian crisis at its borders. Yet a few weeks later, Merkel would radically change position. After months of claiming that she could not open her country's borders – months of trying to find a cross-EU solution to the number of migrants amassing on Europe's borders – Merkel welcomed hundreds of thousands of migrants into Germany. With her actions, encouraged and counselled by the EU President Jean-Claude Juncker, Merkel had hoped that Germany taking the lead would enable and encourage other European nations to follow. By the end of the year, however, the media narrative had changed – Merkel was now synonymous with a doctrine of open borders, a scapegoat throughout the European media for a soft touch on migration. For the right-wing media, she had put European culture and society in danger.

Today, some four years on from Merkel's fateful decision, it is perhaps the refusal of other European nations to follow Germany's lead that makes her welcome seem so remarkable. Merkel's failure to create a cross-EU migration policy was spurred by the refusals of the union's member states. In the UK, for example, the then Prime Minister David Cameron refused to engage with the thousands amassing in Calais. Poland, famously, has, to date, not taken a single refugee. Meanwhile the burden fell disproportionately on the countries of southern Europe – Greece, Italy and Spain. The failure of the EU to propose a coherent policy began to polarize and divide Europe. The EU, with a population of 500 million people, a GDP of $19 trillion and one of the most advanced political structures in the world, was becoming undone due to the pressure of hundreds of thousands of migrants at its borders.

The images presented by the media of migrants making their way across the Mediterranean to Greece and Italy or by land to Bulgaria, shaped popular reactions to these events across the continent. In particular, the media representation of two events gripped public attention. The first was the sinking of a boat carrying more than 500 migrants off the coast of the Italian island of Lampedusa in October 2013, in which some 360 migrants are estimated to have been killed. The second was the death of Alan Kurdi, a young Kurdish boy whose body, washed up on a beach in Turkey, was immortalized in a photograph that made front pages of newspapers across

Europe and across the political spectrum that September. These two iconic mediatized moments stand out because of the extent to which they shifted public opinion; with the benefit of hindsight it is clear to see just how short this moment of 'empathy' would last.

This volume, *Lost in Media*, represents an attempt to challenge the fundamental displacement of voices in the European media. A collection of essays, this book brings together the thoughts and voices of leading writers, journalists, thinkers, and artists, many of whom are of migrant and refugee backgrounds, to consider how migrant perspectives sit within the public sphere, and how to supersede the cliché-heavy, problematic lenses through which migrants' lives are all too often presented. For us, the displacement, and loss, of these voices in the pan-European media sits at the very root of Europe's current crisis.

Migration remains at the heart of the European predicament. The European media, however, have systematically failed in their coverage of these issues. Migrants are represented in the European media in extreme binaries, as either vulnerable or as dangerous outsiders. If they are present in media coverage, they are merely seen as statistics or represented as silent actors, never as authors of their own stories. Many journalists fail to tell the full story. Frustratingly often, the media give little context as to why migrants have been coming to Europe, or how situations in their countries play into these movements, or indeed how European foreign policies play a role in creating these movements. Neither is there a great deal of reflection on the media's own role in worsening the discourses and debates that poison so much of our politics. Migrants may have entered European societies but they are rarely heard from and largely absent in the public conversation that exists around these issues.

Since 2015, EU states have continued to squabble over the legality of search-and-rescue missions in the Mediterranean. Time and time again, the EU has failed to deal with the humanitarian crisis on its borders. Rather than view the plight of people on the move across the Mediterranean as a humanitarian issue that required search-and-rescue operations, the EU instead has chosen to militarize its borders and build vast systems to keep migrants out. Meanwhile, in its member states immigration remains the defining political issue in Europe today – an issue that has disordered political systems across the continent. The toxic debate around migration played an important role in sweeping the far-right populist Matteo Salvini to power in Italy. In the UK it drove the vote to leave the EU. In the days leading up to the referendum, the anti-European political party UKIP unveiled a poster that used one of the most famous images of the migrant crisis, of migrants at the Slovenian border, captioned with the words 'breaking point'.

In this age of illiberalism, it appears that the founding principles of the European project – set up by luminaries of the post-war era in response to the havoc and violence of two world wars – may be at risk. 2019 marks 30 years since the Berlin Wall fell and 15 years since eight eastern European nations fulfilled the promise of 1989 in joining the EU. Today, Poland, the Czech Republic, and Hungary are governed by populist far-right politicians that seek to use the crucial European elections in May 2019 to advance their cause in the European Parliament. While Merkel waits for her successor to take the reins as Chancellor, in France, the liberal hopes pinned on President Emmanuel Macron after his victory over the far-right Marine Le Pen in 2017, have been shaken by the populist *gilets jaunes* protests.

Lost in Media seeks to explore this complex terrain. As the award-winning journalist and author Daniel Trilling argues in his essay, the European media's depiction of the migrant crisis is a starting point for the uncomfortable reality of the present situation. In the years since 2015, the media and politicians have drawn upon a deep well of racism, xenophobia, and Islamophobia as a way to argue for hard borders and nationalism rooted in the rejection of those labelled as 'non-Europeans'. Undoubtedly these stereotypes feed off ignorance and our current climate of misinformation, as editor Antonija Letinić discusses in the context of the Balkans. For her, education has a positive potential and profound importance in responding to these otherwise intractable issues. At the same time, it is important to reflect that this is a game the right has played for many years. As the journalist Dawid Krawczyk shows, Poland's current right-wing government drew great strength from a two-decade-long culture war over art deemed offensive by politicians – a culture war that Krawczyk links directly to the current administration's attitude towards migration. This age of illiberalism has ushered in, for many, a sense of pessimism. For the acclaimed performance artist and activist Tania Bruguera, the danger is that this pessimism leads to inaction. For Bruguera, the great danger is that we get too tired to keep up the fight.

The question of *who* gets to tell migrant stories sits at the heart of the volume. The liberal media have at times played a negative part in the exclusion of migrant voices, as writer and *Guardian* newspaper columnist

Nesrine Malik argues. The preoccupation with stories of 'good', 'virtuous' migrants feed liberal biases, while more nuanced, complex stories of migrants remain buried beneath the azure waters of the Mediterranean. In conversation, two of the world's most important writers, Aleksandar Hemon and Nadifa Mohamed, discuss the realities of their displacements, from Bosnia and Somalia respectively, and the complexities of telling their stories and the stories of people like them. For Hemon and Mohamed, their work as authors of fiction offers them latitude to tell such stories. As the *El Diario* journalist Moha Gerehou argues, racial stereotypes populate Spanish media to an extent that limits any real form of representation for migrants – or indeed non-white Spanish citizens – in the public sphere.

Of course, the migration question is rooted in deeper European histories. These are histories that are denied as often as they are forgotten; histories of colonialism rarely discussed. Europe has all too often refused to confront its history of brutal racism and how colonial plunder and globalist mass extraction are woven through the stories of migrant arrivals from Africa and the Middle East today. It's no coincidence that migrants come to Italy from Eritrea, Somalia and Libya, all of which were once Italian colonies, but as the Turner-Prize-winning artist Lubaina Himid says in conversation, there's a 'collective amnesia' over the colonial legacies of Europe and how these histories are woven into migration today. Her work testifies to these issues. Such a history is balanced, too, by that of the exile, as discussed by the renowned writer Ece Temelkuran. Like many writers before her, Temelkuran is no longer able to live in her home country, Turkey. She did not make the journey by sea, and her situation is far more secure than that of many; yet she remains displaced, lost amidst the claims made on her and the heavy weight of the designation: 'exile'. As André Wilkens, the director of the European Cultural Foundation, writes in order to change media narratives that frame migrants as strangers or a threat, we need a European public sphere that is democratic and in which diverse perspectives can be shared equally.

The publication *Lost in Media* is the culmination of the European Cultural Foundation's two-year-long Displaced in Media project that sought to find ways to challenge media discourses around migration. The project, which the European Cultural Foundation's Menno Weijs explains in detail in the book's afterword, worked with young migrant filmmakers across eight European countries, and grew out of *Remapping Europe* and its companion volume *Remixing Europe*. The book includes stills from some of the Displaced in Media films, featuring the work of Anonim, Jade Jackman, Roda Abdalle, and Mulham Muhammed Hidel. Elsewhere we have also used images from the American artist Jacob Lawrence's iconic 'Migration Series', which tells the story of black migrations in America, and photographs the internationally renowned photographer Jillian Edelstein took of migrants on the Greek island of Lesvos.

Taken together, these responses – both visual and written – show us that in these troubling times, as Tania Bruguera reminds us, we must not get tired but rather build common bonds of experience. The media have a unique role to play in fostering such engagements and building shared values by giving space to migrants and refugees to tell their own stories. Every year marks some sort of milestone or turning point but 2019, with its anniversaries of the fall of the Berlin Wall, eastern European EU accession and the likely paradigm-shattering EU elections – not to mention the dénouement of Brexit – represents a vital moment to consider the stories we tell about Europe and its citizens. For us it is only through radically reforming the discourses around migration – by recognizing the personhood of displaced persons and recognizing the power of their stories – that the European public sphere can begin to find answers to the crises the continent faces.

A note on definitions: Refugee or Migrant?

Refugee or migrant? Does it matter? We feel it does. Describing people as refugees has become politically charged; yet it remains too narrow to adequately describe the scale and diversity of people on the move. Throughout the volume our contributors refer to 'refugees', 'migrants', 'asylum seekers', 'newcomers', 'racialized people' – though to be clear these things often have different, at times even opposing meanings.

As Daniel Trilling writes in his essay, definitions of 'refugees' or 'migrants' reduce complex stories of people on the move to singular types that may feed our liberal bias but render many on the move invisible. Likewise, as Aleksandar Hemon argues, for many refugees who struggle to get the legal rights they deserve under international law, their legal designation as such remains critical. In this volume we have let our diverse contributors set their own terms in their discussions of immigration in all of its forms and complexities.

Like many of the other people I met, as a journalist who spent several years reporting on displaced people's experiences at the borders of Europe, Caesar was surprised at the lack of understanding, even indifference, he felt was shown to people in situations like his.

Daniel Trilling

Like many of the other people I met, as a journalist who spent several years reporting on displaced people's experiences at the borders of Europe, Caesar was surprised at the lack of understanding, even indifference, he felt was shown to people in situations like his.

Daniel Trilling

Jillian Edelstein, *Life Seekers*, 2018, photograph.

Jillian Edelstein, *Life Seekers*, 2018, photograph.

Uncomfortable Facts

The Migrant Crisis in the European Media

— Daniel Trilling

In 2015, as the refugee crisis in Europe reached its peak, I was visiting a friend in Sicily. Caesar had arrived there the year before, rescued from an inflatable boat that was drifting in the Mediterranean. Originally from Mali, he had spent eighteen months being passed from trafficker to trafficker in Algeria and Libya, and had suffered all the hardships that journey entails. In 2015, he was still getting used to his new situation: sitting and waiting while his case made its way through Italy's asylum system; occasional bursts of frustration as he wondered if he should try his luck elsewhere in Europe; trying to keep the memories of torture and abuse at bay, as he looked for a way to get on with his life. Whenever we talked, I could see that he was feeling a kind of culture shock. Like many of the other people I met, as a journalist who spent several years reporting on displaced people's experiences at the borders of Europe, Caesar was surprised at the lack of understanding, even indifference, he felt was shown to people in situations like his. Didn't Europe know why people like him were forced to make these journeys? Hadn't Europe played an intimate role in the histories and conflicts of countries like his own?

Caesar watched television and he read the newspapers, and he didn't like the way people were being portrayed; particularly the constant distinction made between the deserving and the undeserving. 'It's not as if one person has "refugee" printed on his forehead and another has "economic migrant"', he told me on more than one occasion. He noticed too, how attention seemed to flit from one place to another and how some people's stories were treated with more urgency than others.

When I visited him in late August 2015, it was the week that thousands of people were making their way through the Balkans, towards Austria and Germany, and when I arrived at Caesar's house, he was watching footage of people – mainly from Syria, Afghanistan and Iraq – crowding on to trains at Budapest's Keleti station. 'You see?' he said to me. 'The cameras don't come here anymore because it's only blacks arriving in Sicily now.' Caesar felt strongly that even among refugees, the media valued some lives more than others.

Europe's refugee crisis, or more properly, a disaster partly caused by European border policies, rather than simply the movement of refugees towards Europe, was one of the most heavily mediated world events of the past decade. It unfolded around the edges of a wealthy and technologi-cally developed region, home to several major centres of the global media industry. Scenes of desperation, suffering, and rescue that might normally be gathered by foreign correspondents in harder-to-access parts of the world were now readily available to reporters, news crews, filmmakers and artists at relatively low cost.

The people at the centre of the crisis were, at least for a time, rela-tively free to move around once they had reached safety and to speak to whoever they pleased. This gave certain advantages to the kind of media coverage that was produced. Most of all, it allowed quick and clear reporting on emergency situations as they developed. Throughout 2015, the crisis narrative was developed via a series of flashpoints at different locations within and around the European Union. In April, for example, attention focused on the smuggler boat route from Libya, after the dead-liest shipwreck ever recorded in the Mediter-ranean. A month or so later, focus shifted to Calais, where French and British policies of discouraging irregular migrants from attempting to cross the English Channel had led to a growing spectacle of mass destitution. By the summer, the number of boat crossings from Turkey to Greece had dramatically increased, and images and stories of people stepping onto Aegean shores, or of piles of orange lifejackets, came to dominate. Then came the scenes of people moving through the Balkans, and so on, and so on.

In all of these situations the news media were able to do their basic job in emergency situations, which is to communicate what's happening, who's affected, what's needed the most. But this is usually more than a matter of relaying dry facts and figures. 'Human stories' have the greatest currency among journalists, although it's an odd term if you think about it.

What stories aren't human? In fact, it's most commonly used to denote a particular kind of human story; one that gives individual experience the greatest prominence, that tells you what an event felt like, both physically and emotionally. It rests on the assumption that this is what connects most strongly with audiences: either because it hooks them in and keeps them watching or reading, or because it helps them identify with the protagonist, perhaps in a way that encourages empathy, or a particular course of action in response. As a result, the public was able to easily and quickly access vivid accounts and images of people's experiences as they attempted to cross the EU's external borders, or to find shelter and welcome within Europe.

The trade-off was that this often fit into pre-determined ideas about what disasters look like, who needs protection, who is innocent and who is deserving of blame. Think, for example, about the most recognizable image of the refugee crisis in 2015: the picture of a Turkish police officer carrying the lifeless body of three-year-old Alan Kurdi away from the water's edge on a beach near Bodrum.

As the Dutch documentary *Een zee van beelden* (*A Sea of Images*) (Medialogica, 2016) asked: why did this image in particular strike such a chord? After all, many news editors see images of death on a daily basis, yet for the most part decide to exclude them. The documentary showed how the apparently viral spread of the Aylan Kurdi photograph on social media was in large part the result of a series of decisions taken by senior journalists and NGO workers.

First, a local photo agency in Turkey decided to release the image to the wires because they were so fed up with the lack of political response to the crisis on their shores. The image was shared by an official at a global human rights NGO with a large Twitter following, and retweeted by several prominent correspondents for large news organizations. Picture editors at several newspapers then decided, independently of one another, to place the photo on the front pages of their next editions; only after that point did it reach its widest circulation online. The image gained the status it did for a mix of reasons – political, commercial, but also aesthetic. One of the picture editors interviewed in the documentary commented on how

Daniel Trilling

the position of the figures in the photo resembled that of Michelangelo's *Pietà*, an iconography of suffering and sacrifice that runs deep in European culture. But if this way of working has its advantages, it also has its dark side.

News media that rush from one crisis point to another are not so good at filling in the gaps, at explaining the obscured systems and long-term failures that might be behind a series of seemingly unconnected events. To return to the idea of a 'refugee crisis', for example, this is an accurate description in one sense, as it involved a sharp increase in the number of people claiming asylum in the European Union; from around 430,000 in 2013, according to the EU statistics agency Eurostat, to well over a million in 2015 and 2016 each.

In global terms this was a relatively small number of refugees: the EU has a population of over 500 million, while most of the world's 68.5 million forcibly displaced people are hosted in poorer parts of the world. But the manner of people's arrival was chaotic and often deadly, while there was a widespread institutional failure to ensure that their needs – for basic necessities, for legal and political rights – were met. To stop there, however, risks giving the false impression that the crisis was a problem from elsewhere that landed unexpected on European shores.

This impression is false on two counts. First, Europe has played a key role, historically, in the shaping of a world where power and wealth are unequally distributed, and European powers continue to pursue military and arms trading policies that have caused or contributed to the conflicts and instability from which many people flee. Second, the crisis of 2015 was a direct effect of the complex and often violent system of policing immigration from outside the EU that has been constructed in the last few decades.

In short, this has involved the EU and its members signing treaties with countries outside its borders to control immigration on its behalf; an increasingly militarized frontier at the geographical edges of the EU; and an internal system for regulating the movement of asylum seekers that aims to force them to stay in the first EU country they enter. This, cumulatively, had the effect of forcing desperate people to take narrower and more dangerous routes by land and sea, while the prioritizing of border control over safe and dignified reception conditions compounded the disaster. How well, really, did media organizations explain all this to their audiences?

The effect, all too often, was to frame these newly arrived people as others; people from 'over there', who had little to do with Europe itself and were strangers, antagonistic even, to its traditions and culture. This was true at times, of both well-meaning and hostile media coverage. A sympathetic portrayal of the displaced might focus on some of those images and stories that matched stereotypes of innocence and vulnerability: children, women, families; the vulnerable, the sick, the elderly.

Negative coverage, meanwhile, might focus more on the men, the able-bodied, nameless and sometimes faceless people massed at fences or gates. Or people from particular countries would be focused on to suit a political agenda. *The Sun*, one of Britain's most widely-read newspapers, for example, led with a picture of Aylan Kurdi on its front page in September 2015, telling its readers that the refugee crisis was a matter of life and death, and that the immediate action required was further British military intervention in Syria. A few weeks later it gave another refugee boat story the front page, but in contrast to the earlier one the language was about 'illegals' who were seeking a 'back door'. This time, the refugees were from Iraq, and they had landed on the territory of a British air force base in Cyprus, which legally made them the responsibility of the UK.

The fragmented and contradictory media coverage of the crisis left room for questions to go unanswered and myths to circulate: who are these people and what do they want from us? Why don't they stop in the first safe country they reach? Why don't the men stay behind and fight? How can we make room for everyone? Are they bringing their problems to our shores? Do they threaten our culture and values?

One of the first people I met in the course of my reporting was Azad, a young Kurdish man from northern Syria, in a hastily constructed refugee camp in Bulgaria at the end of 2013. At the time, the inability of Bulgarian and EU authorities to adequately prepare for the arrival of a few thousand people – the camp, at Harmanli in southern Bulgaria, marked the first time Médecins sans frontières had ever set up emergency medical facilities within Europe – seemed like an unusual development.

Everyone was new to this situation, and the camp's inhabitants, largely Syrians who had fled the war there but decided that Syria's neighbouring countries could not offer them the security they needed, were shocked at what they found. Several of them told me that this couldn't possibly be the real Europe, and that they would continue moving until they found it. Azad was friendly and wanted to know lots about where I came from,

Daniel Trilling

London, and to find out what he could about the other countries in Europe, and where people like him might find a place to settle.

I went back to meet Azad several times over the next two years, as he and his family made their way across Bulgaria, and then Central Europe, to Germany. During that time, the backlash against refugees grew stronger, a fact Azad was keenly aware of. In Sofia, in the spring of 2014, he pointed out places in the city centre where homeless Syrians had been attacked by street gangs. Later that year, in eastern Germany, we walked through a town where lampposts were festooned with posters for a far-right political party. By the autumn of 2015, Azad and his family were settled in Germany's Ruhr area, and he was much warier of me than he had been in our early meetings. He could see that hostility ran alongside the curiosity and welcome that had greeted the new arrivals to Europe; and he knew how giving too many details away to journalists could threaten what stability people in his situation had managed to find. Within a few months, a series of events – the ISIS attack in Paris in November 2015, the robberies and sexual assaults in Cologne that New Year's Eve – had provided the excuse for some media outlets to tie well-worn stereotypes about savage, dark foreigners and their alleged threat to white European purity to the refugees of today.

The most brazen of these claims – such as the Polish magazine *w Sieci*, which featured a white woman draped in the EU flag being groped at by the arms of dark-skinned men, under the headline 'The Islamic Rape of Europe' – directly echoed the Nazi and fascist propaganda of Europe's twentieth century. But racist stereotyping was present in more liberal outlets too. The *Süddeutsche Zeitung*, in its coverage of the Cologne attacks, prominently featured an illustration of a woman's legs silhouetted in white, with the space in between taken up by a black arm and hand. Racism is rooted so deep in European history that at times like these it can remain unspoken yet still make its presence clear.

Now, several years on from the peak of the refugee crisis, we are faced with a series of uncomfortable facts. The EU has tried to restore and strengthen the border system that existed before 2015 by extending migration control deep into Africa and Asia. The human rights of the people this affects, not least the many migrants trapped in horrendous conditions in Libya, are taking a back seat. Far right and nationalist movements have made electoral gains in many countries within the EU, and they have done this partly by promising to crack down on migration, to punish refugees for daring to ask for shelter from disasters that Europe was all too often the midwife to. Politicians of the centre are being pulled to the right by these developments, and a dangerous narrative threatens to push out all others: that European culture and identity are threatened by intrusions from outside. If we come to view culture in this way – as something fixed and tightly bounded by the ideologies of race and religion, or as a means for wealthy parts of the world to defend their privilege – then we are headed for further, greater disasters.

The irony is that you can only believe in this vision if you ignore not only Europe's history, but its present too. Movement, exchange, new connections, the making and remaking of tradition – these things are happening all around us, and already involve people who have been drawn here from other parts of the world by ties not just of conflict but of economics, history, language, and technology. By the same token, displacement is not just a feature of the lives of people from elsewhere in the world; it's been a major and recent part of Europe's history too. And what has kept people alive, what has preserved traditions and allowed people to build identities and realize their potential, is solidarity: the desire to defend one another and work towards common goals.

  If there is a failure to recognize this, then the way people are represented by our media and cultural institutions has to be at fault, and setting this right is an urgent challenge. This isn't only in terms of how people are represented and when, but who gets to participate in the decision-making; who gets to speak with authority, or with political intent, or with a collective voice rather than simply as an individual.

All too often, the voices of refugees and other marginalized people are reduced to pure testimony, which is then interpreted and contextualized on their behalf. One thing that constantly surprised me about the reporting on refugees in Europe, for instance, was how little we heard from journalists who had connections to already settled diaspora communities. Immigration from Africa, Asia or the Middle East is hardly new to Europe, and this seems like a missed opportunity to strengthen bridges we have already built. Though it's never too late. Zainab, a woman who fled Iraq with her three young children in 2014 and who I met later that year in London, once told me how surprised she was at people asking her why refugees came to the UK.

Daniel Trilling

I would like to answer back', she said, 'hasn't Iraq been occupied by Britain and America? I want people to see the suffering that the popu lations from these places have gone through. I really wish for people to see the connection.

The more those of us who work in media can help people to see connections such as these, the more I think we can break down the idea of irreconcilable conflict over migration. Because, really, there is no 'over there' – just where we are.

Jillian Edelstein, *Life Seekers*, 2018, photograph.

Jillian Edelstein, *Life Seekers*, 2018, photograph.

"You see?," he said to me. "The cameras don't come here any more because it's only blacks arriving in Sicily now." Caesar felt strongly that even among refugees, the media valued some lives more than others.

Daniel Trilling

"You see?" he said to me. "The cameras don't come here any more because it's only blacks arriving in Sicily now." Caesar felt strongly that even among refugees, the media valued some lives more than others.

Daniel Trilling

There I was, the only black guy on the team. As plain as the nose on one's face, a difference not really worth mentioning.
However, that's just not how reality works and, like other teammates with whom I share blackness, I had to endure racist incidents of one kind or another.

Moha Gerehou

Moha Gerehou, *The most racist advertisements in history*, 2018, 5.19 min.

Moha Gerehou, *The most racist advertisements in history*, 2018, 5.19 min.

A Prophesy Fulfilled

Race and Migration in Spain

— Moha Gerehou

As the clock struck the first fleeting second of the year 2000, hundreds of doomsday prophecies were already headed straight for the trash. Seconds, minutes, hours and days passed, and yet the new millennium didn't cause the end of the world and with it, the extinction of human beings predicted by some. In the end, speculations collapsed in the face of facts: life would go on, as beautifully and horribly as ever.

For me, that was not just any year. Not because humans had managed to survive the turn of the millennium (I hardly cared and barely understood), but because I had just signed up for one of the local football teams in my city, Huesca. Nearly 8 years old and with young legs, I was as excited as any other kid in the world who dreams of being a footballer.

There I was, the only black guy on the team. As plain as the nose on one's face, a difference not really worth mentioning. However, that's just not how reality works and, like other people on teams with whom I share my blackness, I had to endure racist incidents of one kind or another.

They say that history repeats itself in cycles with similar structures and different actors. For me, that time-cycle came back around later, in the year 2012 and the Mayans declared that humanity would perish on 21 December. I was studying journalism in Madrid that year, and lived with the Mayan prediction but also with other, more ominous forecasts – which, for me, were objectively much worse, because they predicted nothing less than the end of journalism. Years later, a fellow journalist with many years' experience under his belt told me he'd never known a time when journalism said everything was okay. The arrival of social networks and the shift from print to digital reading signalled natural changes that, in the words of the pontificators – coincidentally, those who'd always worked in print – would surely be the death of journalism. Those people keep on pontificating as if nothing happened, which I think is a joke.

It has always been clear that the Internet and social networks heralded a new way of doing things, an unprecedented scenario that forced the old-guard media to make a choice: update and adapt, or die. This opening also gave new media a chance to carve out its own niche, more or less success-fully. This is how eldiario.es appeared around 2012 where three years later, I joined a relatively new team for its short journey, above all for its pioneering partners system and its vision of journalism.

But once again, there I am: the only black person. What's more, there are people who call me the 'black guy at eldiario.es', or say that they hired me for being black in a show of modernity and a nod to diversity, as if my curriculum vitae read only: 'Moha Gerehou. Black'. I sincerely don't take these comments to heart; the purpose they do serve for me, though, is to encourage deeper reflection about journalism and its profound importance in the narrative of reality. The first comment is obvious, as it's still strange to see black people in the media, while in other areas it's absolutely normal. Correct me if I'm wrong, but not once in my life have I heard anyone in front of a group of construction workers shout something like, 'Hey look, it's the black guy in construction'. There are places where we are expected and others where we are intruders, and the media are among this second group. Most of all, we should know what prevents black people from being part of the media when we are an active part of society. Basically, we must question where that ceiling is and who put it there.

Lucía Mbomío, a journalist from Radio Televisión Española, told me that the presence of black people inside public and private broadcasting sectors had barely changed. She has been in the field for more than ten years and is an example of a black journalist who has succeeded, but the focus must shift to the reasons why Lucia's presence is an exception and not the rule. Whenever I pass by schools, I am struck by the great ethnic and racial diversity, which really shocks me given the panorama I lived in at university. We were four black people; one in my group was nicknamed 'the fake Moha'. What I am getting at is, how come all of the diversity present in the compulsory stages of the education system doesn't transfer to higher education. We must also address the lack of examples in media, a result of the prior point. People with similar life histories in those positions can help enhance visibility for a part of society that never sees itself reflected.

Finally, there are the barriers to access ranging from difficulties in finding employment as a migrant, through the wall of Spain's 'Aliens Act', to the invalidation of knowledge acquired in their countries of origin, especially from the Global South. Many migrant women who work as cleaners have completed higher education in their home countries, but in Spain they are not given the opportunity to use their degrees. Academia and institutions invalidate and reject that knowledge for not having been achieved according to their standards and perspectives. This is a tragedy with grave repercussions, as it condemns people to greater precarity.

History is written by the winners, and these mostly tend to be men – white, straight, and economically powerful. Chimamanda Ngozi Adichie adroitly explained this problem in her TED talk 'The Danger of a Single Story'. You need only glance at the executive management of Spanish media, almost always led by people with this profile, to see an example. This problem can't be examined from just an economic viewpoint; the analysis must also undertake a critique from the perspective of the racial, sexual, gender and all those historically excluded and marginalized identities and realities.

Discrimination can greatly hinder one's arrival, and it's not as if it's easy once you do arrive. A study published in 2016 by the *Guardian* hit the nail on the head. After compiling all of the comments posted on its website since 2006, they concluded that of the ten accounts that suffered the most harassment, eight accounts were women (four white and four racialized) and two men, specifically blacks. In addition, within that Top 10 there were three homosexuals, one Muslim and one Jewish person. The great paradox is that the majority of account holders were white men, heterosexuals and, to name a religion, Christians, but none of these were among the top ten most harassed.

In that same year of 2016, I uploaded a photo to Twitter that sparked a heated controversy on social media. I was on my way to work and while passing through the Plaza Mayor (Madrid), I came upon a rally of veterans with their flags and uniforms, calling for the street to remain named in honour of Millán Astray, an icon of the dictatorship and ideals of Francisco Franco. The Madrid City Council decided to eliminate this military reference in the capital city's street map, a change that these reactionaries were not going to stand for. When I saw the scene, I took a selfie and

Moha Gerehou

uploaded it to Twitter with the caption: 'The face you make as you pass a group of veterans calling for a street to be named for a Francoist.'

What followed that tweet was an unprecedented level of violence directed towards me. On top of the usual criticism of anyone defending the Law of Historical Memory was added a racist violence beyond all levels. My message was by no means among the greatest stands against a fascist demand, but what I got back in return perfectly illustrates how, when I air my political opinions in the media, they are being linked to the racial issue. Much of the questioning directed my way wasn't because I supported a measure that was considered 'left-wing', but because as a black person I had an opinion on a political issue that affected Spaniards. Although I was born in Huesca, my blackness is not equated with Spanish-ness because of a monolithic, stale concept of what it means to be Spanish or European, a space exclusively reserved for whites. Here are five real examples of the shots fired:

'Shut up you ingrate, you know nothing about Spanish history, if you don't like it go back to where you came from.'
'Yeah right, you idiot, like we don't have enough already with half the country criticizing the other half, we need you to come and make jokes.'
'At least they're Spanish – you're not.'
'When are you going to talk about the mass rapes in northern Europe by Islamist refugees?'
'What the hell do you know, deadbeat, go back to your country and live the dream.'

This same logic applies to what happens in the media and to interactions with readers or viewers. I remember that in my early days at eldiario.es, when I was writing on topics for the economics section, some comments left for me on social networks went far beyond the disagreements and criticisms abounding in similar texts, and went on to directly attack me as a black person of migrant origin. The same thing happens both inside and outside the newspaper with those feminists who dare to appear in the media, whether with gender related discourses or not. The challenging questions and violence to which they are subjected always focus on their state as women, imposing the constraints of patriarchy on them. Columnists like Barbijaputa in eldiario.es, or the women of *Afroféminas* or *Pikara* magazine have come to know this reality all too well. Faced with this reality in the media, what do we have left? Nowadays the presence of the different realities and identities forming our entire society has a greater weight in the public debate. This is something feminism especially encourages, like the initiative #LasPeriodistasParamos, but other questions arise that should be put on the table. How can we ensure, as much as possible, that racialized people and migrants can enjoy media space without being subjected to the violence that puts us in the crosshairs?

The well-rehearsed speech the media has ready about their struggles against the pressure bearing down from political and economic powers, which are transformed into concrete initiatives, must also incorporate their vision of a response to pressure from racist, sexist, and homophobic powers. Otherwise, the media ends up being just another way to toss us into the lion's den. From initiatives that eliminate all hiring barriers to those that seek to end harassment in the newsroom, to finding a way to guarantee freedom of expression, we do our journalism or occupy media space. We must reflect and above all act to guarantee the full expression of the rights of those facing different forms of discrimination. This means both re-examining existing initiatives and applying a more comprehensive approach to all that lies ahead. The latter reminds me of a conference organized by a progressive foundation in order to discuss 'Journalism and Migration'. There were many recognized journalists who do great work and have unquestionable track records, but two omissions really stood out for me. First, there were hardly any migrants anywhere at the event, and the few migrant attendees had jobs that were focused not on the Spanish state, but instead mostly related to situations in other countries. The second was that, basically, there were no journalistic initiatives led by and presented by migrants. I can think of the websites EsRacismo, Afroféminas or Afrokairós, to name but a few good examples.

The gravity of the problem is that today, when it comes to migrants and racialized people, media space is made available only when we are the subjects of research, but not to present us as the owners of our own political identity. Even when we are occasionally portrayed as such, from a global perspective it's a drop in the ocean. Every time an Islamist group claims a terrorist attack, the media presence of Arab and Muslim people instantly increases. The modus operandi is usually the same: if the Muslim population wants to be freed from association with the terrorist acts, they must proclaim loudly and clearly that they do not side with terrorism. This brings up several issues. First, it is those who are guilty of an attack, indirectly or not, who should be trying to escape blame for their act, not those who share some trait (in this case, religion) with the perpetrators

Moha Gerehou

41

of a massacre. Otherwise, the entire Muslim population is found guilty, with nothing left to do but publicly beg forgiveness in the eye of the media.

Secondly, in practice Arab and Muslim people are only present as experts in the media when there are terrorist attacks. The rest of the time it would be very difficult, if not impossible, to find a woman in a *hijab* appearing in a debate on the economic situation, or offering her opinion on Catalan independence. Their space in the media is reduced to the racial, migrant, and religious condition, almost always as victims or executioners, leaving little room for their role as subjects capable of communicating beyond race, origin, or religion. Intersectionality is not a concept, and diversity is not an objective. Instead, both are existing realities and if they are not represented socially, the reasons can be traced to an underlying history rooted in discrimination. I mention this because in my few years as an activist in the anti-racism struggle, all we hear are promises and pleas for patience because things are going to change.

There are prophecies to be made but especially to be fulfilled, and in the debate on the future of the Spanish media, that process remains incomplete. It has to be put on the table: journalism must be diverse in order to better reflect a diverse world. I am convinced that journalism always warrants the use of a perspective that is as broad as possible in order to show the full picture; to be rigorous, truthful, faithful to reality and critical of abuses committed by all forms of power.

Solutions can only come from a collective debate starting with some basic outlines that will become more complex along the way, both to think about and to establish in society. Media whose professionals are a true representation of society, without economic, racial, or gender barriers. A media strategy that takes all of these considerations into account while never losing rigor. Results that uphold the classic pillars of journalistic standards and broaden access to knowledge and information for all of society while not ignoring other fundamental rights. In a context where rights and freedoms are more at risk than ever, journalism is more necessary than ever as one of the greatest monitors of power and guardians of the right to freedom of expression.

Back when I stood not even a metre high, the first prophecy marked me as the only black man on the team. Years later, the second prophecy foretold the future of journalism. The third prophecy must come from uniting both visions into one, bringing the racial issue together with journalism to create a just society at all levels. It is in our hands, in the hands of the media and institutions to really put it on the table and make it happen.

Moha Gerehou, *The most racist advertisements in history*, 2018, 5.19 min.

Moha Gerehou, *The most racist advertisements in history*, 2018, 5.19 min.

The gravity of the problem is that today, when it comes to migrants and racialized people, media space is made available only when we are the subjects of research, but not to present us as the owners of our own political identity.

Moha Gerehou

The great contradiction
is our capacity to remain
preoccupied with the legacies
of war, while remaining
completely oblivious to the
sufferings of people who have
faced similar experiences
and face a similar fate.

Antonija Letinić

The great contradiction
is our capacity to remain
preoccupied with the legacies
of war, while remaining
completely oblivious to the
sufferings of people who have
faced similar experiences
and face a similar fate.

Antonija Letinić

Mulham Mohamed Hidel, *It's not hard*, 2018, 5.41 min.

When I moved to Istanbul it was the biggest step in my life

because I left my school and my friends and my town

Mulham Mohamed Hidel, *It's not hard*, 2018, 5.41 min.

Fake News and Fake Facts

**Media Literacy and Civic Engagement
in the Balkans**

— Antonija Letinić

A few months ago, I picked up a newspaper whose headline read, 'Migrant kills wife'. On closer inspection, what kept my attention was the lead explaining that the migrant was a person from Croatia. At a time when the news is full of headlines describing the criminality of migrants and refugees, I found this twist subversive.

In the late summer of 2015, newspapers, web portals, TV and radio programmes were flooded with the 'unexpected' wave of refugees attempting to enter the European Union. First they were passing from Turkey to Greece, then across Macedonia and Serbia, Bulgaria and Hungary. When the Hungarian Prime Minister Viktor Orbán closed his borders, intimating he would build a wall, a project of insanity – as if walls can stop people, as if we have a right to prevent people's movements – refugees were redirected towards Croatia. In those early days we were able to follow the movement of people through our country pretty much live in the media. We also tracked how the then government behaved. Mostly, we were pleased with the humanity shown by state officials, the organization of the police and the infrastructure provided by the state, as well as the behaviour of citizens preparing food, sanitary goods, clothes and necessities; all those things that people deprived of home and security need most in their search for a safer future. Whether the behaviour of the state representatives was encouraged by the upcoming elections at the time or by pure humanitarian motives may be up for debate, but from the current position it doesn't seem important. What we remember are the images of police officers holding children in their arms and taking care of them. What we listen to and watch now are the new reports on the deaths of refugees in their attempts to cross borders, on violence and racist backlash.

In the autumn of 2015, the media were broadly aligned in their support of refugees and launched initiatives to provide them with help, supporting campaigns by Refugees Welcome, Are You Syrious?, Jesuit Refugee Service and the like. The Croatian context should be kept in mind: Croatia is a small and homogeneous culture with few minority members – the ones who are part of society are mostly historical minorities so the fluidity of the population is somewhat limited. The whole region of ex-Yugoslav countries is intertwined by ethnic, national, and religious tensions that rise and fall depending on the political constellations in each country. Sometimes it feels as if every few years we are on the verge of a new war, with threats at the border and constant provocations. Although the last war, provoked by the dissolution of Yugoslavia, ended almost 25 years ago, in the past few years it has seemed as if it hasn't ended, or threatens to start up again. Somehow, we haven't managed to grow beyond this conflict. The great contradiction of this is our capacity to remain preoccupied with the legacies of the war, while remaining completely oblivious to the sufferings of people who have faced similar experiences and face a similar fate. The legacy of conflict has been to keep the former Yugoslav states as closed cultures with poor economies and dim prospects for the future.

This reality has made Croatia, like the other countries in the region, only a passageway rather than a destination for many refugees. The small number of asylum seekers that have found their way to Croatia in the past indicates that we have weak and underdeveloped programmes for integration and a low visibility of multiculturalism in society compared to the larger and more diverse states of the EU. To state some facts: since the introduction of the programme for asylum seekers and subsidiarity protection in 2006, Croatia has granted 739 international protection claims; 600 asylum claims, and 139 subsidiarity protections were granted. Although the number of granted claims has increased substantially in the past few years, Croatia, compared to other EU members, remains restric-tive in the approval of international protection; and a less desirable destina-tion country due to a poor quality integration system. As a result, migration and refugees have a limited presence in the country's media, whether as subjects of discussion or voices listened to. Migrants are represented in a generalized perspective in stereotypical and predictable ways. Furthermore, when migration is discussed, it is only in relation to scandals, breaches of rights, felonies and violence. In the radical right-wing media, the picture is even darker. Refugees are represented as a threat – to national security, to culture, to stability and to religious tradition. Over the past few years, since the start of the 'migrant crisis', it has been interesting to see how and which media presented information about migrants and refugees, especially those provoking fear, encouraging intolerances and antagonism through misinformation. These articles usually rely on questionable sources, hiding publishers and authors. They are often media with a reputation for fake news.

Fake news is intentionally distorted information that is published in media, blogs, and social networks with the aim of deceiving audiences and manipulating them. Fake news is usually built on partially correct and credible information, but these stories often disguise or hide their sources, which makes it harder to fact-check them. As a rule, fake news has one main advantage compared to factual information: creativity, and primarily addressing the emotions of its audience. In this lies the answer to the question of how is it possible for fake news to pollute the media landscape so efficiently.

Antonija Letinić

As a new branch of journalism, fact checking always sounded to me like a red alert. I liked to think that somehow it would be the starting point of journalism rather than something new and specialized. Well, this is the point where we find ourselves in the history of journalism – the picture of decline is clearly drawn.

The statement that the traditional media have finally reached the point of no return is a valid one, and yet, it has been made many times before, without consequence. The media are still here, news is being produced, new platforms emerge, the number of new outlets keeps increasing. So, when considering the state of the media today, what can we consider to be different from moments of crisis in the past? First of all, when we talk about media in a traditional sense, we continue to think about newsrooms and outlets that have a huge impact on society, political dynamics and public opinion. When I look at younger generations, however, those of my niece and nephew, my colleagues' and friends' children, but also drawing on experience from our students in Kulturpunkt's Journalistic School who are mostly in their early twenties, I see that they just simply do not read newspapers, they don't watch central television news programmes, or to put it simply: they don't consume media in the same way nor do they perceive the media in the same sense that previous generations did. In that respect, we do not necessarily know, nor can we foresee, how the traditional media will change or transform in the decades to come. Famously, the emergence of radio was considered as a threat to newspapers, just as the emergence of television was considered a threat to radio; the Internet, of course, was considered as the fatal blow to all media – and yet none of these formats have died. What happened instead was not terminal, but a fundamental change of structure. Each new format of media changed the way news and content are produced, placed, and advertised; and none more so than the Internet, which transformed our consumption of media from something linear to something completely non-linear. Indeed, the emergence of radio and radio formats over the past few years was enabled by digital technologies. Today, audio books are the fastest growing segment of the digital publishing market, while e-books are taking an increasingly larger share of the publishing sector at the same time as the market for printed books is growing. YouTube channels, YouTubers, and social media influencers can gain a greater audience than some traditional outlets, but the traditional outlets have not faded away.

Drawing the landscape in this way gives us a blurry image of the future of the media where we can't see precisely what will happen to the media specifically, but more importantly to society in a broader sense. Fake news is polluting media in all their forms and appearances. Fragmentation and specialization of the media is dispersing audience and its impact. Fundamentally the only way to arm ourselves against this shifting and uncertain future is to look to new forms of media literacy. Today it is gaining more and more relevance, and has been recognized on the political level. But what is to be taught and how?

Since 2013 we have developed a media literacy module within the framework of the Kulturpunkt's Journalistic School. The programme is dedicated to young authors and future journalists who wish to gain a better insight into contemporary cultural and artistic practices. We focus on newly emerging, engaged, and critical practices that can be seen as a prism through which we can consider society and the processes that evolve within it. The arts have always had the capacity to reflect on the contemporary moment, to detect the flaws and feebleness of any time, to anticipate future currents and offer rich and diverse perspectives. Wishing to offer to our students as broad a perspective as possible we present lectures that explore the framework and dynamics defining the media next to series of lectures in contemporary culture and arts. The programme segment we developed dedicated to media literacy introduces them to the structures of the media, the transformations they are experiencing, how content production has changed, the different forces shaping pressure on the media, market and political influences. An important part of the module relates to critical reading, understanding how media operate and how they place information and for what reason. Especially nowadays, with the increase in fake news, distorted representations, and biased reporting, critical competences are essential.

The problem is that so much of the news remains shaped by the traditional perspectives of the media. Today we need something more, something else. The more knowledge we acquire, the more important it seems to approach media literacy in a completely different way. The Displaced in Media project attempted to do precisely that; to use all possible aspects of media literacy and more.

To educate, to better understand the media system, to involve a wide range of media formats, and where possible encourage youth to use them, to create their own language, produce their own content, to share, distribute, and participate. We can't necessarily influence big media systems, and indeed it shouldn't be our aim, especially with such limited resources and capacities, to transform the giants. If we instead focus on the small scale, perhaps, like the butterfly effect, we can have a big impact. Giving voice to migrants and refugees, to the marginalized and deprived, primarily in the sense of offering them tools and skills, can have a much greater impact in the long run. As we look out on an increasingly uncertain century it is clear that the skills of the journalist are now the skills of the good citizen. Media literacy is necessary for true civic engagement in the coming century.

We most probably can't stop fake news, manipulation, and distortion. Combatting them will probably remain the main goal of the media in the coming decade, and in that sense the audience will be the media's main partner in this combat. For this reason, we need media literacy as a tool to help us build our relationship with the audience, to equip them with relevant knowledge and methods for detecting scams and lies. Without a relevant and credible media, it is hard to imagine a functional and just democracy.

Have we already lost this battle? Many election results seem to point in that direction, but if we lost a battle – it doesn't necessarily mean we have lost the war. In that sense, we shouldn't leave the field too soon, but rather think of new strategies of how to approach this game of inequality and demand more democracy at all levels. The hope for our future is to be found in education, and in our communities. Communities in which everyone is a journalist.

Mulham Mohamed Hidel, *It's not hard*, 2018, 5.41 min.

If you believe you can do it, just do it.

Mulham Mohamed Hidel, *It's not hard*, 2018, 5.41 min.

The problem is that so much of the news remains shaped by the traditional perspectives of the media. Today we need something more, something else.

Antonija Letinić

The problem is that so
much of the news remains
shaped by the traditional
perspectives of the media.
Today we need something
more, something else.

Antonija Letinić

The difference between
an immigrant and a refugee
in my mind is the amount
of agency that one has.
The reason I couldn't claim
the status of refugee is
because I chose not to go
back, I chose to stay,
just as I, under different
circumstances, had chosen
to leave.

Aleksandar Hemon

Jacob Lawrence (1917–2000), *The Migration Gained in Momentum,* panel 18 from *The Migration Series*, 1940–41.

Jacob Lawrence (1917–2000), *The Negro press was also influential in urging the people to leave the South*, panel 34 from *The Migration Series*, 1940–41.

Agency and Displacement

— Aleksandar Hemon in Conversation with Nadifa Mohamed

Nadifa Mohamed and Aleksandar Hemon are two authors with a background of displacement. Mohamed, a British-Somali novelist, was born in Hargeisa (now in the Republic of Somaliland) and moved to England as a child, staying permanently when war broke out in Somalia. Hemon left Bosnia in 1992, before the outbreak of war, for the United States, where he has lived ever since. His books include *Nowhere Man*, *The Lazarus Project* and *How Did You Get Here? Tales of Displacement*.

Nadifa Mohamed Can I ask you a question, Aleksandar? Do you still feel displaced?

Aleksandar Hemon I do, yes, but I am also learning to live with it productively and, I guess, learning not to be traumatized by continuous displacement. One important thing in this whole equation is the distinct possibility that the sense of displacement is rooted in an experience that is inherently traumatic. This is clearly the case for refugees fleeing war, but I think that even voluntary emigration – that is, when people get up, sell their property and move to a new place – even that contains a certain amount of trauma.

Trauma is inherent in displacement; there are different degrees and intensities, and obviously for war refugees it's the highest possible amount of trauma. I was not thrown out of my house, so violence, direct violence, is not part of my displacement – really in some ways I was never a refugee. One can sometimes overcome trauma and it was relatively easy for me to do so. So, I am displaced but I have found forms and ways, including writing, in fact primarily writing, in which that displacement is productive and not perpetually traumatic.

NM You left on a pre-arranged trip to the US before the war, right?

AH Correct, yes.

NM Likewise, my family left Somalia two years before the war to join my father who was already living in the UK. So that idea of whether I'm a 'real' refugee or not is something that comes up regularly – people want me to be a refugee sometimes because it brings a kind of romanticism to my life story. But I'm also quite insistent on being described as an immigrant, even though I was four years old when we moved and so I had no control over it, but I was joining my father who was already an economic migrant. I think that distinction is important. Still, you leave a place thinking it will still be there when you return, and that was something I strongly believed as a child. I thought we were only in the UK temporarily and then in 1988, less than two years after we left, there was no country to return to, and I guess it must

have been a similar case for you, with Yugoslavia.

AH It was, yeah. The difference between an immigrant and a refugee in my mind is the amount of agency that one has. The reason I couldn't claim the status of refugee is because I chose not to go back, I chose to stay, just as I, under different circumstances, had chosen to leave. That difference was very stark in the 1990s when there were people being thrown out of their homes and killed. I had no right to claim that because I was able to make choices. I remember specific times and moments, indeed, when I had to choose whether to go back or to stay? A refugee, a migrant who's fleeing violence, doesn't have that choice. When I left, Slovenia and Croatia were already independent, so although there was a state that called itself Yugoslavia, the original shape of it that I had grown up in had already gone. So, I was already making peace with that reality, and in some ways, I was leaving a country that didn't exist yet, which is Bosnia. When I left, Bosnia was not independent. That took place while I was in Chicago, in the first few months of 1992. This is not to correct what you were saying at all, it's rather to point to the fact that it's very hard to establish uniform moulds for the refugee or displacement experience. Everyone has a different experience. Everyone comes from the same space, as it were, Bosnia, Somalia, but the experience is still theirs, and still they are so different and so particular, even in the tragic sense, that it really is difficult to generalize. I always have to footnote whenever people ask me anything about my experience of Bosnia, Yugoslavia and about my relationship with that – I don't know what it's like for you but I cannot give simple answers to any of those questions. To me it's everything – I just keep talking because there's always more to say. It's more complex that anyone assumes.

NM Absolutely. When I went to Sarajevo over the summer for the book festival, it was upsetting to me; it was quite – I don't want to say traumatizing – but it made me think about a lot of things that I hadn't thought about for a long time. I went to a museum that had an exhibition on the Srebrenica massacre and seeing all of the names listed, one after the other, so many family names connected to each other, made me think about my family and the uncle I lost in the war – the only one who died violently – but also about the others who died because of epidemics in refugee camps and other stupid, awful reasons. Experiencing it all

vicariously from the UK, I didn't understand it at the time, and the easiest way was just to not look at it. But what I found in Sarajevo was that there is a huge desire to look, to keep looking, to not look away, while in Somaliland it's the complete opposite – there's one kind of shabby memorial in the city centre of a plane that was shot down during the war and is now on a plinth – but otherwise there are no museums and no-one talks about the war. The only real thing to mark the war is the number of mentally ill people and private clinics to deal with them. So, seeing Sarajevo respond to that trauma made me think more clearly about the trauma that my family have experienced.

AH That's very interesting. I'm not sure why there was that response. I know that as soon as Sarajevo came under siege, there were already people, including some involved in the government, thinking ahead, collecting data and recording what was happening with a view towards the future.

They were already thinking what Sarajevo would look like after the war and how the war would be remembered. They were collecting evidence to document what were self-evidently war crimes and they were already preparing for the future history and the future legal redress.

Aleksandar Hemon | Nadifa Mohamed

NM So that started immediately?

AH In some ways. The Srebrenica massacre of course happened in 1995, by which time the world had been watching what had been going on in Yugoslavia. So, it was at this stage shocking to many Bosnians – this was the privilege of Bosnia being, at least geographically, in Europe. People believed that the world would not let something like this happen in Europe. The Sarajevo Olympic Games had happened just eight years before. There was a sense of Sarajevo being a worldly city. Bosnia is in Europe, but the victims were Muslim and so they were not quite in Europe. The Bosnians were watching themselves through other people's eyes to some extent, and as a result they were keeping those records. They were already invested in the images of the city before the war. I watched it, a lot of it, I mean not the killing obviously but the siege, the diplomatic games around it, the reports, it was all on TV all the time.

NM And how aware of the build-up to war were you, the build-up to it when you were there?

AH Well it's a strange thing. I worked as a journalist and that was all we covered, though I was a culture editor. A lot of my friends – to this day they are my friends –

were straight-up journalists who would go and report on political issues, including the war. My roommate, a very close friend, went to report on the war in Croatia when it started and as a result was detained and nearly killed. I remember the magazine I worked for activating their journalistic association in Bosnia and sending faxes to save him. When he came back a few days later he had bruises all over his body from where they had beaten him. The larger picture was horrible. As more things were broadcast, it was easier to see what was going on. At the same time, the strange thing is – similar to our experience in the United States right now – that people will not believe what is happening as it is going on. What I learnt is that you have to imagine that something is real for it to be real, and this applies to things as they are happening, because people think 'this cannot be happening', 'this is not real', and therefore they cannot see what is in front of them. I think it's partly a mechanism of self-protection; we do not want to imagine our death every day of our life because if we did, we'd go crazy. I kept thinking, 'This cannot happen, because what would I do if it happens?' It's hard to imagine an alternate reality from within our present reality, and the total disintegration of reality is difficult to imagine too.

NM Personally, I find such things very easy to imagine. I think I've always lived on high alert. I've always believed that my life is precarious, my existence is precarious, and that's something I've inherited from my mum, who didn't want to leave Somalia, war or anything, she didn't care. That was where her roots were and she had no desire to leave them, so when she came to the UK, she felt like her life would disintegrate here. I had a strong sense of that too, and with the situation in the US today, I think it's affected me so deeply that I've hunkered down – I know what this is and I know how much it threatens me and it's one of the reasons I've not been back to the US for two years. I'm too frightened.

AH I understand. I think that people negotiate their reality depending on how or where they are and how they are exposed to it and where they might be in their life or geographically and socially. I often think about how I called my parents in Sarajevo a couple of weeks before the siege ended. While talking to my mum on the phone I would hear shooting and my mum would say, 'Well, they are already shooting less than yesterday!' She kept expecting things would return to normal, that there would be a correction, but, of course, it cannot happen. The thing that

is most frightening to me in the United States in many ways is this perpetual, vast, public hankering for a correction – that somehow Trump and Trumpism will be corrected by an investigation, or an impeachment, or whatever, some kind of correction and everything will go back more or less to how it was before. It is a total fantasy.

NM Yes, and I think that is what is different having come from a place like Somalia where things have been bad for a long time, but everything has had a short life. So, the dictatorship had a relatively short life. The colonial period was relatively short, so there is a sense that everything eventually collapses. The US hasn't had a collapse like that since the Civil War. I think that people don't realize that there is more violence in America than there is in Somalia. The number of mass killings in America completely exceeds anything that people would associate with the most war-torn parts of Africa. So, if that's your normal, where do you go from there?

AH What I'm worried about is not actually a civil war here in America, but the displacement and violence in society, and the disintegration of societal infrastructures. Society increasingly functions as a bunch of bubbles, which undermines the

69

whole civic project, in which some kind of common civic order is imaginable. But this is reaching the point, and this is familiar to me – I don't know what your experience of Somalia was – where people's agendas are mutually exclusive. There is no way to negotiate a shared outcome. I do not negotiate with fascists personally. I don't advocate that.

NM There's a really nice passage in your piece about Kemalemir Frashto[1] where you say, 'What literature does, or at least can do, is allow for individual narrative enfranchisement. The very propo-sition of storytelling is that each life is a multitude of details, an irreplaceable combination of experi-ences which can be contained in their totality only in narration. I take it to be my writerly duty to facilitate the telling of such stories.' That really resonated with me. I don't think of myself as having a particular goal with writing but this feels close to it.

AH Thank you for saying that. I mean, this project that I'm doing, it's really a justification. Because, I'm sure, you meet Somalis all over the world, I meet Bosnians...

NM Yes, this completely felt very familiar, this conversation you had with Frashto.

AH ... and I asked him, 'How did you get here?' I was asking him just as conversation ... so, tell me about yourself. For migrants, displaced people, the question, 'Who are you?' cannot be asked without asking, 'How did you get here?' People who have always lived where they are, in their native space or home space, you don't ask them, 'How did you get here?' You don't ask that of a Brit or of an American.

NM How did your paths cross?

AH Someone told me about him when I was talking about the idea before it was a project, they gave me his contact details and I called him. What I discovered in doing this project, and it does support the passage that you read, what is really fascinating to me is the desire of people to tell their story. It's happened more than once, including Kemalemir, that people would say to me, 'I've never told the whole story to anyone', or, 'I've never told anyone this part'. Because a lot of people would tell parts to various people but they would never achieve a complete narrative. I don't know if his was complete but, for him, there was this desire to complete the story – I had to do very little prompting – and every once in a while he would say, I forgot to tell you this, and then he would fill in that part. Sometimes they would leave things out because they were uncomfortable or private and personal but they had that part in their head, I could see. There is a basic narrative structure to a migration story: you start over there and then you end up over here. So, people often told me what happened chronologically but even with that they would skip a part and then go back to it because they would have a sense of incompleteness of the narrative. To me it always meant two things: one of them was this desire, even if it had to be controlled or checked, to complete the narrative, to tell the whole story, and also, in relation to that, that it was a form of agency, that telling the story and telling the *whole* story, was at least an imaginative attempt to own it. To me, everything we're talking about – the difference between immigrants and migrants and refugees and people who are in their home space – I think it can be measured with levels of agency. To think of a war refugee as someone who has the smallest amount of agency – that's someone who cannot choose when to leave, how to leave, what to take, how to stay alive, because someone is trying to kill them. To me, migration is really driven by a desire to move into spaces where people will have greater agency. You're trying to survive – but not only to survive but go to a place where you would have a chance and space and ways to make a decision about what you want to do in your life, about what to do with your children. To me, this striving to me is the most fascinating and poignant and tragic thing in describing what is happening to migrants. But some of that agency is reimagined by people by telling their stories. They were recalling their choices, they owned their agency in their narratives. At the time it might have looked like they had no choice – it was random, it was just luck. But when we narrate, we make choices, what to tell, what not to tell, how much to tell.

NM What do you think about how those experiences are translated between writers and readers who have never experienced anything like that? What happens to the writer who's trying to mediate that?

AH Well, it's tricky. In the 1990s, when I lived in Chicago, there were a lot of Bosnians who arrived, serendipitously, in my neighbourhood, so I would run into them. I also met people who were involved in a project at the University of Illinois that was dealing with trauma and addressing trauma by way of testimonial. I'm paraphrasing a vast project by experts, you know, but basically the idea, as I understood it, was that for traumatized people, whether individually or collectively, one of the symptoms or situations common in that trauma is a very strong sense of disconnection from the outside world, from the world outside of the trauma. In a very basic sense, that is, no one who has not experienced what they had gone through could understand what that experience was like. And the consequence of that, and I've seen it, was that traumatized people hang out together because they can understand one another better, but it also means that they can never escape from their traumatic states because everyone is telling the same stories about rape and murder and shelling, different in details but not structurally. So, this whole project was trying to help those people get out of their trauma, as it were, by providing them with a space or way to testify about what happened. Not just for legal purposes, but to tell someone outside the space what happened and to allow them to develop a belief, a sense, that someone outside the space could begin to understand and would care. Now, it's very possible that no one could ever fully understand what happened to someone who was inside that space but the leap between total inability to understand, to someone who might be able to at least try to understand, is huge. So, I had to deal with that leap from inability to being able to listen. I understood the language, I knew the people, I knew the geography, I knew the details of the war. I was as close as can be to that space and yet I was outside. One of the things I learned – this was in my twenties – I learned to listen to people, which I wasn't good at when I was young.

NM What you are saying makes me think about one of my recent obsessions, the Grenfell Tower fire. You have this tower of social housing which was 80% Muslim, 90% immigrant, it was a tower of displacement, of people displaced from other parts of the world. I've been going through all of the witness statements for the enquiry – there are dozens of them, of people who lived in the tower and survived the fire but lost family in the fire. They range from a man who had fled from Eritrea and had multiple degrees but was now living and working in London as security guards. There was another guy, from Afghanistan, who had been a high-ranking army official and had fled the Taliban. There were all of these incredible narratives, mostly ending in tragedy, in London, in the richest borough in the country. One thing that comes through in a lot of the narratives is a strong sense of survivor's guilt, of people who kept thinking, I should've knocked on more neighbours' doors, I should've rung when I left, people who had really little agency in that moment but are now destroying themselves because of the guilt that they still carry. The sort of space Grenfell represents I'm very familiar with, it's similar – I didn't grow up in such an international place, I was on an estate in South West London which was very English – but it still feels very familiar to me and as an adult it's definitely been my world. And I notice that we're not writing about that – *I'm* not writing about that world, I've been concentrating on what happened in Somalia and have been going through these old wounds and ignoring what's been happening right in front of me in London, where people can burn to death in a tower because they've been neglected and they're neglected because of who they are and because of the narratives told about them. So, I feel a real discomfort now with literature, with the way I've been working, with the way that I've been understanding things – it's felt like a real shock to the system.

AH That's difficult. But there's always a sense of obligation and duty – the ethics of writing that you are now expressing – that to me is familiar. It doesn't come to fiction writers naturally. When I wanted to be a writer in my twenties in Sarajevo, I wasn't invested in finding ethical ways to engage with the world by way of language and literature. At the same time, I had read writers for whom the ethics of literature was really important. Those were not the only writers I read but it was part of the literary culture in eastern Europe. Dissidence and, you know, the politics of it was always present. Then that was all reactivated by the war in Bosnia. I started thinking about it in that present context. The point being, and I don't mean to be presumptuous about your work in any way, that you could think about Grenfell Tower because you were thinking about Somalia.

NM Yes, I think they're closely connected.

AH As regards this ethical question, the ethical issue, the ethics of literature, what it does and what it doesn't do, what it can do, what it can't do, you are nowhere near failure in that respect. People have extremely productive and fruitful lives without ever addressing the actual ethics of literature. For us, it seems to me, it's ever present, inescapable. It's not something you wake up in the morning and think: now I'm going to do ethics.

NM One of the funny things

73

about the process of becoming a refugee is that it often throws in the victims of violence with the perpetrators of violence, so that's why in the US there's been a long-ongoing case of a torturer from the Somali dictatorship who moved to Minnesota where many Somali refugees are, and so former political prisoners brought a case against him. It became a very high-profile case because it had an impact on what might happen to other such people in the US. I've been thinking about this a lot. I am particularly interested in societies that have ruptured. So even with my first novel, without knowing, I was actually kind of trying to map all of the ruptures that had happened to Somalia because of colonialism, because of the Second World War, and the second one was set just before the Civil War and the first few days of it in Somalia. The novel I've just finished now is set in Cardiff in a part of the docklands, which were completely demolished in the late 1960s and don't exist in the same way at all any more. There's something in me that keeps going back to those societies that are on the edge, I think, and that has definitely contributed to my feeling that the society I live in, the one that is familiar to me, is also very fragile and could disappear.

AH Well yes, there are fewer people in that society who actually know that because they believe in some kind of inherent property of society that is going to keep it stable forever, despite all historical evidence and the evidence they have right now.

NM Yeah, and I think Britain is particularly bad for that. All of the jingoism, the whole national myth is that we could never be anything but great.

AH I suppose. I also think that with societies like the British and American ones – so dependent on the belief in their special value and exceptional qualities – what they are becoming incapable of is changing before it's too late. Because they think this everlasting constitution, this everlasting quality of our people, will just correct everything. Whereas we know, one way or another, that it can all just collapse, just like that, because it can. There's really no rational reason to believe that it can't. So, the question is how long it will take and what it will take. People think and everyone thinks and I think that way because the constitution of human psychology is that you imagine only what is the extension of this reality, or you're more likely to imagine the extension of what you already know. To imagine the unimaginable is obviously not possible but it is the unimaginable that changes the world, not the imaginable. It's the discontinuity that's frightening and discontinuity is what is going to end Great Britain, not the continuity. It becomes kind of a logical, conceptual paradox. To imagine a different place, you have to imagine a different place, not this place just slightly different. For some reason that's very difficult for people and I think this is where fiction comes in – the perpetual practice of the imagination. We live as humans and as writers, not only past lives and present lives but also our possible lives. We edit possible lives. I don't want to be presumptuous but you have your character or situation thinking maybe he or she could do this, or that, and then you make choices, you make ethical and narrative and imaginative choices based on what hasn't happened yet. So, in that sense, pushing the society to its limits is often done, usually done, imaginatively, in narratives. That is the exciting thing about writing. I think people like us, who are displaced and also coming from somewhere else, are not in awe – I have never been in awe – of that great stability of American or British society and Western civilization. To me, that was never self-evidently present.

NM To me neither. It's interesting because for Somalis in the 1990s,

it was much easier to get asylum. You could fly here, you didn't have to cross the Sahara or risk your life across the Mediterranean, people just landed at Heathrow and gave themselves up as refugees. There was a huge influx and my family were on the fringes of it because most of the people settled in East London or North London and we happened to live in a place where other Somalis didn't. I've been looking at it now and it was such an incredibly traumatic time. There were many suicides, there were people living on thirty pounds a week and then sending fifteen pounds of that back to their family, wherever they might be. It's not a surprise to see variuos dysfunctionalities within second-generation and third-generation Somalis and I do believe that it's because of the trauma of that period. The whole idea of refugees being accepted I think was a bit more popular in the 1990s but was still very marginal. I grew up in an area where you would see far right stickers and graffiti and the rest of it. It's easy to really think of the past as being simpler than it is now but it wasn't. This whole idea that Britain, I think, has an open hand towards refugees, that's not true. The US as well, when there were Jewish refugees in the 1930s and 1940s, most of them were not allowed in. Some of them were sent back. It leaves

Aleksandar Hemon | Nadifa Mohamed

me feeling that if you're a refugee you're only good for filling in the gaps that society wants you to fill in – as cheap labour, as someone to feel good about, as a receptacle of mercy and charity. That's not enough to build an identity on and I wonder about young people who seem very keenly aware of the fact that they don't belong here and they reach for Islam, they reach for other things but there's nothing that can really assuage that feeling that, deep down, they're not wanted here.

AH For a lot of immigrants and migrants and refugees – there is this trauma that they were expelled from one place because of who they were and now they are not received in another place because of who they are. Even if it's relatively welcoming, the wound of trauma is so sore that it's very difficult to just settle into this, which is so different, we have to constantly explain ourselves to other people and justify our presence here. And I am white, I am a man, I speak English, I write in it, and still I have a constant need to explain myself to people who do not know me. To this extent, I do not belong here, I am not self-evident here. For someone who comes from a different background – I mean, I could fit, I could somehow merge, but I could never be self-evident.

NM You could be invisible.

AH What happens to African refugees coming in now or people coming in from Guatemala – their children's children will have to be explaining themselves.

NM Yes, and I still feel like I'm explaining. My family have been in the UK since 1947 and I still feel that I'm marginal, that my grip on society is still very tenuous. It's a scary thought.

AH I think it's productive intellectually and for a writer, but it really is difficult. I, for one, I have an outlet in which I can address that. I have a domain of agency.

NM Yes, me too.

AH But there are people who don't – the people in Grenfell Tower.

NM Exactly.

1 Aleksandar Hemon, 'Gay, Muslim, Refugee: On Making a Life in Trump's America: Aleksandar Hemon Tells the Story of Kemalemir Frasht', from *The Displaced: Refugee Writers on Refugee Lives*, ed. by Viet Thanh Nguyen (New York: Abrams Press, 2018), avaiable on https://lithub.com/gay-muslim-refugee-on-making-a-life-in-trumps-america/.

Jacob Lawrence (1917–2000), *Race riots were numerous. White workers were hostile toward the migrants who had been hired to break strikes*, panel 50 from *The Migration Series*, 1940–41.

Jacob Lawrence (1917–2000), *One of the main forms of social and recreational activities in which the migrants indulged occurred in the church*, panel 54 from *The Migration Series*, 1940–41.

I still feel like I'm explaining. My family have been in the UK since 1947 and I still feel that I'm marginal, that my grip on society is still very tenuous.

Nadifa Mohamed

Here in Poland, the country that is the most ethnically homogenous country in Europe, the ruling party have managed to use the threat of a 'refugee invasion' as an extremely productive tool to mobilize their political base.

Dawid Krawczyk

Here in Poland, the country that is the most ethnically homogenous country in Europe, the ruling party have managed to use the threat of a 'refugee invasion' as an extremely productive tool to mobilize their political base.

Dawid Krawczyk

Anonymous, *Anonymous*, 2018, 4.06 min.

Polish people also remember the crimes

done by Ukrainians in Volhynia.

Anonymous, *Anonymous*, 2018, 4.06 min.

First to Feel Offended, First to Offend

Two Decades of Poland's Culture Wars

— Dawid Krawczyk

On 18 June 2018, Dominik Tarczyński, an MP from the right-wing Law and Justice party (PiS), shocked the world. Maybe that's an exaggeration, but he definitely shocked Cathy Newman, the presenter of the UK's *Channel 4 News*, who asked him, live on air, if he felt a sense of shame when he thought about 'a hundred unaccompanied children, seven pregnant women adrift on a ship, on the Mediterranean while politicians argued'. Tarczyński stuttered in response, 'Well, first of all, the shame should be feeling present within the parents who are, in my opinion, I would say, immature. They shouldn't take their children, they shouldn't be there. They shouldn't put their children at risk by violation of the regulations.'

'But once they are in that situation, don't the politicians of Europe have a moral, humanitarian duty to step in?' Newman continued.

'No', was Tarczyński's answer.

'How many refugees has Poland taken?' Newman asked visibly perplexed by Tarczyński's attitude. 'Zero', answered the Polish MP smirking.

Quotes from the interview were printed throughout the European media; it even made some headlines. But the truly shocking thing about the whole debacle was that, in 2018, people are still surprised by statements that are mainstream in Polish political debate.

Some pundits have referred to Angela Merkel's decision to accept tens of thousands of refugees as an 'experiment'. Personally, I'm not sure that providing refugees with asylum is really an experimental move. Bold and unusual certainly, but not really experimental. By contrast, what I have witnessed in Poland since the Law and Justice party took power in 2015, with regard to the refugee crisis, is truly experimental. Here in Poland, the country that is the most ethnically homogenous country in Europe, the ruling party have managed to use the threat of a 'refugee invasion' as an extremely productive tool to mobilize their political base. 'Refugee' has rapidly become a bad word. In political discourse they are the perfect others, who cannot defend themselves as Poland has taken virtually zero refugees. In the Polish political landscape refugees constitute a figure that can be smeared, denigrated, and humiliated, all to serve the political goals of the current government.

In 2019, Poles celebrate the 15th anniversary of their EU membership. The country that in a relatively short period of time emancipated itself from Soviet control, joining both NATO and the EU, is now home to a strange and divisive political discourse in which refugees can be freely denigrated, while those who dare to criticize the Catholic church and Polish nationalism face severe consequences from the state. The roots of this toxic situation go back much farther than 2004, when Poland joined the EU.

In 1999, president Aleksander Kwaśniewski formally signed an agreement with NATO marking Poland's first step to joining 'the West'. Five years later, Poland took the second step by becoming a member state of the European Union. Free press, democratic elections, free market economy, low corruption, and high transparency rates – each and every box had been ticked. The political scene had its own history of conflicts, which went back to way before 1989, but broadly speaking it was divided between liberals and conservatives, with no contemporary left or progressive parties. Poland was the poster boy of the post-Soviet order, telling a flattering narrative for the advocates of Western capitalism. Compared with oligarchic Ukraine or autocratic Belarus, Poland was living proof that free market capitalism and liberal democracy worked.

The campaign for the 2015 elections in Poland brought with it the first signs of a new political culture – one that challenged this positive narrative. 'There are first symptoms of very dangerous diseases in Europe', said Jarosław Kaczyński, the founder of Law and Justice, in a speech on the campaign trail, in the town of Maków Mazowiecki, to the north of Warsaw. This was not a speech about public health; rather Kaczyński was addressing the refugee crisis. He continued, 'Cholera in Greece. Dysentery in Vienna. Different types of parasites, protozoans are not dangerous in organisms of these people, but can be dangerous here. I'm not calling for discrimination, but this is something that needs to be checked.'

Two weeks after his speech, Law and Justice swept to power in a landslide. Of course, by then, no one really remembered what Kaczyński had said about the refugees. Journalists had their hands full with hundreds of far more newsworthy topics to cover in the new post-election landscape. The Law and Justice party instantly tightened their grip on power beyond the boundaries of democracy. A set of bills first paralyzed the Constitutional Tribunal, dismantling the system of checks and balances; the party then made its move on the General Prosecutor's office, public media, and the Supreme Court of Poland (under pressure from the EU, they stopped short of subduing the independence of the court).

These rapid events revealed the longstanding narrative told by the international press of Poland's success to be nothing but a fairy-tale. The media, enthralled to Poland's poster-boy image, miserably failed to present a comprehensive, complicated portrait of the political tensions in the country.

I believe that on that afternoon in Maków Mazowiecki, Kaczyński effectively redefined the limits of free speech in Polish political discourse. What had once been said only in the far-right regions of online forums and message boards became the new mainstream. It happened without raising an uproar of liberal criticism. In the run-up to the elections it was just one of many loathsome events of an unpleasant campaign. As a former Soviet country, battles over the boundaries of free speech are crucial to understand the tensions that have always been present under the surface of Polish political life. In Poland today, certain institutions, values, and even feelings can count on special treatment, while there are others about whom anything can be said without consequence.

A case in point is the scandal caused by artist Dorota Nieznalska's piece *Passion* in 2001. More than fifteen years have passed since a small gallery in Gdańsk put her work on display. Back then, Poland was not yet in the EU (though the process to join the Union was rapidly advancing) and the global political order had just begun the massive metamorphosis that was caused by the US-led 'War on Terror'. Nieznalska's work was first shown to the public in December 2001 when TVN, the biggest private TV station in Poland, came to the gallery to shoot a short feature for the evening news. The news story sparked unprecedented public outrage. Hundreds of people felt deeply offended by Nieznalska's work.

Dawid Krawczyk

What could possible be so offensive? Male genitals and Catholicism. Neither of them would cause offense separately, but exhibiting them together was a recipe for moral panic. Nieznalska had constructed an installation with a TV set playing a looped recording of a man working out at the gym. The physical pain of the self-imposed workout regime was juxtaposed with the bare, realistic photo of a penis symbolically hanging on a cross. Nieznalska's piece was designed as a critical interrogation of the experience of oppression by the male-dominated Catholic Church and the social pressure of having a 'perfect body' fuelled by fitness and the fashion industry. The work was in dialogue with the so-called Polish Critical Art period, which was at its most intense in the 1990s, during the first years of the post-communist transition, and which explored power dynamics with a particular interest in physicality and human body.

After *Passion* was featured in the national news, protesters took to the streets demanding the cancelation of the exhibition. Parliamentarians from the right-wing League of Polish Families joined the moral crusade and brought the work to the attention of the public prosecutor. The resulting trial over Nieznalska's piece lasted almost ten years. The League of Polish Families, which was rooted in the Catholic-National movement, continued to build up its popularity during these years by attempting to prosecute every single perceived criticism towards traditional conservative Catholicism. It was a strategy effective enough for them to form a coalition government with the Law and Justice party in 2006, though it fell apart, along with the whole coalition, less than a year later.

The Nieznalska case fundamentally transformed the nature of the public sphere in Poland and became a blueprint for the attempts to limit free speech, artistic expression, and journalistic freedom in the years that followed. Ten years after the scandal, Zbigniew Owsiany of the regional public prosecutor's office in Gdańsk gave an interview to the daily newspaper *Gazeta Wyborcza*. 'The educational function of this penal lawsuit is letting other artists know that they aren't allowed to do just anything', he said. 'This is a memento. If artists were allowed to do anything, they could shock us every day with things I can hardly even imagine.'

In the years that followed, artists and performers who rejected the idea that blasphemy is an act that should be policed by the Penal Code became an easy prey for politicians elevating their profiles at the expense of controversial art. In 2007, the death metal artist Adam 'Nergal' Darski performed at the music club Ucho (The Ear) in the city of Gdynia, northern

Poland. During his act he tore apart a copy of the Bible, throwing its pages at the audience while growling 'Eat that shit', shouting that the Bible is a 'deceitful book' and the Catholic Church is 'the biggest criminal cult', as his fans set the pages on fire.

In 2008, the prosecutor's office launched an investigation, but decided to remit it shortly afterwards due to a lack of other offended people. Two years later, a group of MPs of the Law and Justice Party filed a similar claim against Darski for defaming the Catholic Church. The outcome was the same. The investigation was launched and later cancelled by the court's decision. In 2011, the investigation was restarted and finally ended up in court, where Darski was acquitted of all charges.

'It is a victory, or at least a step towards a victory. I consider every court decision in my favour as a victory of common sense over superstition, wrongheadedness, and reactionism', commented Darski after hearing the court's decision.

The culture wars in Poland continued into the 2010s. The legal battles against Nieznalska and Darski were a lesson for both sides. Those who wanted to exercise unhampered free speech and criticize the Catholic Church learnt that they should probably prepare to defend their rights in court, or at least before the prosecutor. Perhaps a more important lesson was learned by the other side: trials are expensive and the results are often unsatisfying. If the legal system fails to deliver, it is time to change the strategy.

In 2014, Argentinian playwright Rodrigo García's play *Golgota Picnic* was announced as part of the repertoire of that year's Malta Festival in Poznań. The play criticizes contemporary consumerism, but it also deconstructs the figure of Jesus Christ, portraying him as an anti-social outcast. Soon after the announcement the Rotary Crusade for the Fatherland organized nationwide protests against the staging of García's play. They collected over 60,000 signatures under a petition demanding the cancellation of the play. The police issued a statement admitting that they would not be able to guarantee security on the streets; according to their estimates some 30,000 people planned to show up in front of the theatre.

Following weeks of organized pressure, Michał Merczyński, the festival's director, broke down and removed the play from the repertoire. In response to Merczyński's decision the play was read in more than 30 cultural institutions across Poland. The Rotary Crusade succeeded in taking down the play from Poznań's festival but they unwillingly initiated

Dawid Krawczyk

a country-wide phenomenon. *Gazeta Wyborcza* printed the whole play in its weekend edition. Performances based on *Golgota Picnic* were staged in open venues, in front of theatres, in public squares. While actors were reading the play, protesters often showed up to conduct exorcisms and harass the audience.

The controversy around *Golgota Picnic* constituted an unprecedented event in the recent cultural history of Poland. *Golgota Picnic* was a power struggle that played out in churches, theatres, and on the streets. While it was at first a victory for bigoted Catholicism, it sparked a strong reaction from liberals.

In February 2017 it seemed that the furore over *Golgota Picnic* would be repeated. At the Powszechny Theatre in Warsaw, a Croatian playwright and director Oliver Friljic staged a play called *The Curse*, which was bold in its criticism of the contemporary Catholic Church. The play touched on such painful issues as paedophilia among the priests, corruption, and the Church's involvement in politics. A few days after the premiere, hundreds of protesters turned up in front of the theatre. Religious fanatics, football hooligans, and nationalist politicians chanted prayers together. This time the director of the theatre, Paweł Łysak, put his foot down and refused to cancel the play.

The culture wars are by no means limited to religion. The late-night talk show host Kuba Wojewódzki was subjected to an investigation by the public prosecutor's office to find out if he had 'publicly insulted' the Polish flag, after a segment in which the illustrator Marek Raczkowski put a miniature Polish flag attached to a toothpick into a prop resembling dog faeces. Insulting the flag is a criminal offence in Poland that is penalized under the law with a fine and even up to a year in prison. Wojewódzki weaselled out of the situation by explaining that the controversy was supposed to direct public attention to the issue of dog faeces contaminating Polish streets, and the prosecutor dropped the investigation. During Pride this July, a group of protesters carried an interpretation of the Polish national emblem coloured with rainbow colours. 'It is a profanation of the national symbols', The Minister of the Interior and Administration wrote on Twitter the day after. As he announced this, he demanded an investigation from the public prosecutor, which eventually announced the law was not broken.

Not only flag and the national emblems are protected by law. The national anthem which is mentioned in the constitution, specific bills, and guidelines is also under strict protection. Altogether they define lyrics, melody, and how the audience should behave when the anthem is performed. They are so precise they even instruct men to take off head-wear while singing.

When Jaś Kapela, a leftist poet, performer, and writer, recorded his version of the national anthem and put it up on YouTube it was not meant to test the limits of free speech, or even criticize anyone. Inspired by the fact that the lyrics were written by Polish refugees, Kapela decided to subtly change the lyrics. He wanted to express the solidarity with contemporary refugees fleeing wars in Syria and Iraq. 'Poland has not yet died, So long as we still live. What the foreign power has seized from us, We shall recapture with a sabre' are the first few lines of the national anthem. Kapela's version was: 'Poland has not yet died, So long as we still live. Our poverty is a history, So now we can help refugees.' The public prosecutor launched an investigation and in October 2016 Kapela was found guilty of defaming the nation and, as the judge put it, 'ostentatiously express[ing] disrespect to the nation and the republic'. Following an appeal, he was found guilty again, but this time not of defaming the whole nation, but just national symbols. Kapela believes that justice has not been served and has filed a complaint against the Polish justice system with the European Court of Human Rights.

These cases are just a sample from the most radical or historically signifi-cant examples of the long-fought cultural wars over free speech in Poland that forced artists and authors to stand up for their beliefs in court. The restrictions on free speech in Poland are real – whether imposed by the courts or by the pressure of public protest or both – in particular when it comes to religion and Polish national symbols. At the same time, it seems like Poland is an oasis of freedom for those who shout aggressive slogans against migrants and refugees. Even examples of publicly expressed calls to violent acts are overlooked by state authorities.

TVP Info, a state-controlled TV station, regularly invites the right-wing journalist Wojciech Cejrowski to comment on the news. Following the far-right riots in Chemnitz in August 2018, Cejrowski was blunt on the topic of Muslim immigrants in Germany. 'The secret service should catch all of them and deport them as a threat to national security. They should be isolated as you would isolate someone seriously ill with jaundice', he said. 'They teach their children from day one that if someone does not bang their head on the floor with you, you can beat them up, steal from them, burn them down.' Cejrowski has only once had to explain his remarks

Dawid Krawczyk

91

before the public prosecutor after stating on Radio Koszalin, a local public radio, that 'Ukrainians are rapists and butchers'. The prosecutor decided not to prosecute, writing in a short statement that 'the act does not match the definition of a criminal act'.

Since 2015, the boundaries of what can be said about migrants, refugees, and basically anyone who is not a white, ethnically Polish man, have been pushed to the limit. The only case that raised nationwide attention involved a man publicly burning an anti-Semitic effigy in Wrocław in 2016. Piotr Rybak, who burnt the effigy, while shouting 'God! Honour! Fatherland!' was sentenced to ten months in prison. Shortly after the sentence the prosecutor intervened; the media have since reported that the prosecutor is politically linked to the Minister of Justice. The prosecutor appealed for the punishment to be reduced from imprisonment to community work. The appeal was not considered valid and Pior Rybak went to prison.

Since 2015, a lot has changed in Polish politics. The Law and Justice Party has put conservative Catholics into power after years of electoral failures. October 2015 is thus usually presented as the turning point from democratic liberalism towards populist authoritarianism. Looking at the judiciary system, state-owned media, and the rule of law in Poland today, such an assessment makes sense, but the history of Poland's culture wars shows a more complex picture.

Interestingly, the new government has not automatically led to strengthening the repression around free speech and the loosening of policing for hate-crimes. While the Polish legal system is not based on precedents, the history of rulings matters. The judicial decisions that add up to the body of rulings have been shaped for almost thirty years. When it comes to free speech, both verdicts valuing the freedom of expression over protection of religious feelings and the exact opposite can be found in the courts' archives. All this makes any judge's decision particularly dependent on the cultural climate and political custom. When the law is not precisely defined, the strongest actor gets to decide. Today that actor is the Law and Justice Party and its leader Jarosław Kaczyński. Based on the events of the last fifteen years it is clear who can count on state protection and who can be insulted with impunity. Religious feelings and national symbols have been removed from the public debate. Regarding the rights of migrants and refugees, Kaczyński drew the line very clearly two weeks before the elections, when he compared them to parasites.

Anonymous, *Anonymous*, 2018, 4.06 min.

They told me to go back to Ukraine.
They asked why I was talking in Ukrainian.

At first, I was terrified.

I'm afraid. I sort of feel that it will never end.

That we'll never be accepted here.

Anonymous, *Anonymous*, 2018, 4.06 min.

'Refugee,' has rapidly become a bad word. In political discourse they are the perfect others, who cannot defend themselves as Poland has taken virtually zero refugees. In the Polish political land- scape refugees constitute a figure that can be smeared, denigrated, and humiliated, all to serve the political goals of the current government.

Dawid Krawczyk

'Refugee' has rapidly become a bad word. In political discourse they are the perfect others, who cannot defend themselves as Poland has taken virtually zero refugees. In the Polish political landscape refugees constitute a figure that can be smeared, denigrated, and humiliated, all to serve the political goals of the current government.

Dawid Krawczyk

I realized that it would be interesting to bring together an extremely diverse group that would never naturally meet each other, that would never go to the same political rallies, that have different interests, and ask, if we put all of these people together, can they work together?

Tania Bruguera

Tania Bruguera, *10,148,451*, Hyundai Commission, Tate Modern, 2 October 2018–24 February 2019.

Tania Bruguera, *10,148,451*, Hyundai Commission, Tate Modern, 2 October 2018–24 February 2019.

A Very Long Fight

— Tania Bruguera in Conversation with Ismail Einashe

Tania Bruguera is an acclaimed Cuban performance artist and activist who lives in both Havana and New York City. Bruguera has participated in many international exhibitions and her work is in the permanent collections of many institutions around the world, including the Museum of Modern Art, Bronx Museum of the Arts and the Museo Nacional de Bellas Artes de La Habana.

In 2018 Bruguera was the recipient of the Hyundai Commission for the Tate Modern's Turbine Hall. The work she created is currently titled *10,148,451*, a changing number that corresponds to the number of people who migrate between countries every year, as well as the number of migrants who die in the perilous journeys they make in search of a better life. Routes like the passage of people from Africa via Libya into Italy, one that cost the lives of more than 2,000 people in 2018.

As part of the commission, Bruguera reached out beyond the traditional limits of an institution such as the Tate Modern, bringing together a group called the Tate Neighbours, 21 people who live and work in the area around the museum. The group is diverse and inter-generational, tasked by Bruguera to reimagine how an international art institution such as the Tate can respond to its location by tackling themes of migration, inequality, poverty and climate change. One of the group's first

Tania Bruguera

101

actions was to rename the Tate Modern's Boiler House after local activist Natalie Bell for one year.

In the Turbine Hall itself, Bruguera has created a large heat-sensitive floor. Activated by body heat, when enough people lie on it, the floor reveals the portrait of a young Syrian refugee named Yousef who lives in London (the museum has only released his first name). In order for this to happen, around 100 people need to lie on the floor, together. As such the work challenges museum visitors to work together. The space is filled with a low frequency sound which is unsettling, and in the corner of the space is a room dubbed the 'crying room'. Here Bruguera, in an act of what she calls 'forced empathy', has filled the room with an organic compound that induces tears.

Bruguera's commission at Tate Modern, which opened on 1 October 2018, goes beyond the parameters of socially committed art. Bruguera has created a profound, yet subtle intervention on the global migration crisis produced through a community-driven process and institutional critique. Ismail Einashe spoke to Bruguera at Tate Modern after her show was opened, to discuss the contours of what she set out to achieve at the museum. A few weeks after their conversation, in December 2018, Bruguera was arrested in Havana along with other Cuban artists protesting the Cuban Government's 'Decree 349' which they say will stifle artistic creativity and suppress freedom of expression.

Ismail Einashe Could you tell me a bit about the process of making this commission? Why did you decide to involve local people?
—— **Tania Bruguera** Part of the motivation to do this project came out of the current political, global situation where there is a tendency towards nationalism and xenophobia and anti-immigration. I started to think about what the role of an art institution is in this context. I heard a lot of people blaming globalization for what is happening, so I was interested in the idea of the return to the local. I wanted to ask how an institution such as the Tate Modern, which is so important in setting the trend of conversations internationally, can have the same impact on the people who live next to it. For me this is a way to rethink how culture can be in one place and in another simultaneously. So that was my starting point, and I thought, well, I want to work with people who live in the neighbourhood. I realized that London has a very specific situation, in that neighbourhoods are very mixed. I realized that it would be interesting to bring together an extremely diverse group that would never naturally

meet each other, that would never go to the same political rallies, that have different interests, and ask, if we put all of these people together, can they work together?

So, it was a personal experiment for me because I thought that if this happens here it means it can happen anywhere. We are just an institution, an artist, we don't have the same amount of power that others have. I wasn't sure that it would work to be honest, but now, after months, I realize that it really is something that can happen, and that people need to trust each other more.

I think that the solution for all the problems there are in the world now – well, that is a big claim – but one of the solutions I have found is that if people feel valued in who they are and what they know, rather than being valued for what they have, materially, then a different conversation is possible. It is happening here. Democracy does work but it takes a long time; it's hard work but it's satisfying. An example of it is the selection of Natalie Bell. Every decision made within the group is consensual. When we decided to rename the building, we put it to a vote and had a discussion – that's democracy. When you have a real democracy, the best person does win. And that was Natalie Bell, she was the best of all the candidates by far.

IE We are in the Tate Modern's Blavatnik Building, named after the Ukrainian oligarch Len Blavatnik who made the largest-ever single donation to the Tate Modern. We are seated here on the fifth floor of the building opposite the Boiler House, which now carries the name of Natalie Bell. The Tate Modern honoured Blavatnik for his financial commitment to the most important contemporary art museum in the world. Meanwhile Bell is a local activist who lives next door to the Tate and has 25 years of local activism behind her, but she's never won an award for it. Why was it so important for you as part of the commission to suggest the Tate rename the Boiler House?
—— TB The idea of renaming the building is that it highlighted for everybody – for the staff, neighbours, and visitors of the museum – not only Natalie herself, but the crisis in which we are living, which is a crisis of values. We have a crisis of value in the world where people value celebrity over knowledge. People think that by liking things on social media they are activists, rather than the people who have been doing the work for twenty years anonymously. The renaming is also a call to re-evaluate the social values we're operating from. We've been thinking a lot about the word 'contribution'. We had a discussion about the plaque

Tania Bruguera

103

and about what we would rename, and we wanted to use the word contribution. Right now, contribution is understood to refer to goods, money or time, but it also means the act of working for the good of others. With Natalie we had a great example of someone doing work that deserved to be celebrated.

IE What you've done is actually much more radical than creating just a group, because a lot of socially engaged art just pays lip service to social change, it can feel like an administrative afterthought. But seeing your commission and spending time with you, I can tell that this process you have been engaged in since the start of 2018 feels different, and unique, to me. Why do you think that is?
—— TB It feels different to me too, I have to say. I think the reason is that I've done two projects like this before, so I come into the group with more knowledge and more clarity of what we're doing. It also feels different because when you do projects that are socially engaged, in places where there are no urgencies, you create laboratories to propagate ideas, but at this point in time there is an actual urgency in the country where it is happening, where people are being beaten up for the colour of their skin, because of where they come from; where real fascists are organizing. So in

this moment, which is very sensitive, it almost feels like art is a tool to navigate social and political issues that otherwise are impossible to discuss because people are so polarized.

IE You have long history of campaigning for migrant rights. You have launched an Immigrant Respect Awareness Campaign and you famously launched an International Day of Actions on 18 December 2011, which was then the United Nations-designated International Migrants Day. Yet in Europe today, there's a wave of anti-migrant sentiments. How can art and cultural institutions respond to this tide?
—— TB I think why we're doing what we are doing, and why it feels different, is because at the moment many people are attacking institutions like art. I feel like in times like this, when you are not represented by the government, when voting doesn't matter because the votes aren't even counted properly and who is going to win has already been decided, when all other institutions are not trusted, I feel like we have to protect cultural institutions. That's why the way we work feels different. It's not about critiquing the institution, it's about finding a way to work together with the institution to make it function differently. It's about finding ways to

make it work in ways that are not traditional, perhaps in ways that aren't necessarily the task of an art institution. It is like how, during the war, the Church brought in refugees to protect them – that's not necessarily the Church's direct mission, but that's how the institution had to adapt to the time they were living in.

I think that what art institutions have to do right now is step in and respond. It's no longer about saying 'Oh come and look at this beautiful art'. In terms of the other question about immigration, I agree with you, in terms of the conversation it's a mainstream conversation but it's not being solved. People are trying to solve the housing crisis, or economic problems but with migration there is still victimization, people talk about migrants and refugees as victims, instead of recognizing the natural right of humans to move freely.

The reason why issues around immigration and refugees have not been resolved is that people are profiting from them. There are big industries that profit from immigrants who work for no money. When they have no rights, they can't ask for vacation, pensions, or insurance. Remember in the US at the beginning of the last century they asked Europeans and Mexicans to come over. The problem is that there is an attitude that treats these people as disposable. That's the problem; people are being treated as objects, which are either useful, or not useful. The other thing is if people keep taking the resources of other countries, people are going to keep leaving. If, let's say, Mali has all the resources, and people invest in Mali instead of taking resources out of Mali, you will not have people leaving the country. It's all about why people don't invest, and by invest I don't mean just doing business, I mean invest in the moral, social sense in other countries.

IE Why was it important to have Yousef's image as part of this commission?
—— **TB** In the *Migrant Manifesto* there is a line that says, 'When the rights of migrants are denied the rights of citizens are at risk'. This is why it's so important to defend those who have nobody to defend them. I think it was important to have Yousef's image because his is a story that was never heard. You always hear stories of refugees that are negative. With minority groups, what happens is that if one member of that group does something wrong, everybody has to pay for it – that person represents the totality of the group. When you are in a group that is privileged, if someone does something wrong, they are an exception. What this means is that in groups that are

105

discriminated against you have no right to individuality, you are part of a mass, of a group that has no face and no individual stories, you are all the same. So, for me it was very important to include the history of Yousef, because it's one specific story and it's a story of success that had all the possibilities of going wrong – he was homeless, there were people selling drugs next to him, he had no family, he couldn't speak English – but he made it right. This is not the sort of story we often hear about immigrants, so I wanted to bring in this idea of success. We make his story the story of all of us. There need to be more stories that show us as strong, resilient people. So, I wanted to do that. I also wanted to illustrate the work of Natalie. When we met with Natalie and told her the name of the building, she was so surprised.

IE More than surprised I hear, she was shocked!
—— **TB** And she was modest. But this is typical of people who do things for others. So, when we spoke, I said give me an example of the work you have done, and she gave me many examples and then she told me the story of Yousef, and I thought that's exactly perfect for the subject of refugees. The other thing that's important to the project is the subject of identity, which I think is complex especially when it comes to immigration. Natalie is a first-generation British citizen, her mother is from Vietnam, and her father is English.

I think we need to understand this in all its complexity. Yousef is a refugee. I think it's important to show complexity and also solidarity. I think one thing we need to fight for is solidarity among immigrants, the ones who've made it and the ones who haven't made it. The ones who are privileged migrants and the ones who are under-privileged migrants, old migrants and new arrivals.

That is a critique I have: we need more solidarity. When we talk about the LGBTQ movement, one thing that always strikes me is how it is a movement that goes beyond class. Of course, there are tensions but they were able to cross generations, cross classes, and that's what we need to do in the migrant and refugee movement: we need to go across age, job, class, across the labour etiquette, across culture.

That doesn't mean that we don't understand that the other person is different, it means that you have to go beyond that to have solidarity. So, for me solidarity is what we need right now.

IE What about the traditional left and right splits, do they still matter?
—— **TB** I think that it is a very important moment in the

world – we can no longer be defined as 'right' and 'left'; rather, we must define ourselves as just and unjust. We are moving away from such traditional classifications; for example, in Cuba we have a president who calls himself a socialist but implements neoliberal laws. What we are seeing now, unfortunately, is the result of decades of people misusing politics, or people using politics for their own personal gain. If someone is from the left, you think that you can't criticize them because they are on your 'side', and this makes people blind to what is wrong. You can't build justice while ignoring injustices.

IE In Cuba you have paid a heavy price for your activism; you have been arrested and imprisoned by the Cuban regime in the past. Since President Miguel Díaz-Canel took over from Raul Castro, Cuba has been trying to reinvent itself, even as a place for gay rights.
—— TB I had a conversation with friends of mine about this. They were happy about the change in the law; they didn't care why it had happened. I told them, I want gay marriage, but I want it to be implemented for the right reasons. Unfortunately, the reason for the government's legalization of gay marriage is not because the government is open and progressive but because the country is in economic crisis. They have no money coming in and ultimately this is 'pink-washing'. They want to build an image of a country that is pro-gay so that the gay community comes to the hotels they are building – it has been done to attract gay tourists specifically.

People are getting excited about how things look and not how things work. Gay marriage in Cuba, unfortunately, does not mean that the gay people there are going to have more rights.

There is still a lack of education, and homophobia; there are no rights for trans people and they don't have access to medication. What we need are not things that look good on paper. They say they will change the constitution but really there is no change. They are not allowing artists to discuss the constitution. Everything is very prepared. Politicians today have learned to be cynical.

We are in the era of the headline. When we see something on Facebook and think it looks good, we don't even read the article. We look at the headline and think, 'Oh I get it'. We need rights, not things that look good. I think we need a new movement that is humanist – not about laws, but about justice, not about looking good, but about doing something that takes a long time and is solid.

Tania Bruguera

It's about education. I have a dream that we would have emotional education, not only education that is fact-based, but education that is emotional, because we need to learn how to respond properly to bullying and to insecurity, so we don't continue to have the situation we have today.

IE Today I was reading an article in the *Guardian* that said that since the 1970s 60 per cent of all the earth's animal life, mammals, birds, fish and reptiles, have been eliminated. We have this ecological, political disaster under way and I think something really scary is happening.
—— **TB** Do you know what is scary to me? Right now, we can't afford to get tired, because this is a very long fight. It's not going to end with whether one president gets elected or not. It's going to be a long fight where we are re-evaluating who we are, and what we want society to look like. People can't afford to get tired, and institutions need to do the jobs that have promised to do. It's all about trust. Are we living a political virtual reality? A lot of people know that a lot of what politicians say is not the truth; there are a lot of things happening behind closed doors. So, we need institutional transparency. The people in power need to make it possible for us to trust them again. Who knows, maybe we have arrived at the time where we have no more presidents; we just have joint councils who decide what to do.

Tania Bruguera, *10,148,451*, Hyundai Commission, Tate Modern, 2 October 2018–24 February 2019.

Tania Bruguera, *10,148,451*, Hyundai Commission, Tate Modern, 2 October 2018–24 February 2019.

I have a dream that we would have emotional education, not only education that is fact-based, but education that is emotional, because we need to learn how to respond properly to bullying and to insecurity.

Tania Bruguera

Migrant stories are told like parables, with endings that tie up neatly, reaffirming our faith in mankind, or sounding a warning about what mankind is capable of. These are one-dimensional images, told flat, heavily edited and primarily recounted from the host's perspective.

Nesrine Malik

Migrant stories are told like parables, with endings that tie up neatly, reaffirming our faith in mankind, or sounding a warning about what mankind is capable of. These are one-dimensional images, told flat, heavily edited and primarily recounted from the host's perspective.

Nesrine Malik

Jade Jackman, *Calling Home*, 2017, 3.36 min.

Jade Jackman, *Calling Home*, 2017, 3.36 min.

Humanizing Stories

Migrants and the Media

— Nesrine Malik

Nesrine Malik

'Humanizing' is a tricky business. We are always told that migrants need to be 'humanized' if they are to be accepted, if an effective counter narrative to the populist one is to be written. And so there is now a cottage industry of humanization, a whole sub-genre of reporting and factual entertainment starring the human migrant. In the mainstream media there are documentaries from the migrant trail by sea and land, and Hollywood adapted scripts, by Lena Dunham no less, about refugee stories. On social media there are curated threads, life-affirming stories, short videos cut to go viral about how the story of this one migrant woman will totally renew your faith in mankind. But the message is uniform. There are broadly two things migrants are allowed to be; positive success stories, or objects of pornified pity. They are either drowning children or cheeky entrepreneurs, they are either camp dwellers or restaurateurs, cutting a ribbon on their third site. They are either utterly dispossessed, or Nobel Prize winners.

This is caricature. What they rarely are in these humanizing stories, is complicated, fractured, and profoundly displaced. Their stories are told with a backdrop of an evacuating devastation. Think of the collage of images that accompanies a migrant story. There are buildings collapsed into rubble, parents mourning dead children, starved hollow faces, queues, always queues, in camps, at borders, at processing centres. Once they

117

arrive at a safe harbour, they are invisible unless they somehow distinguish themselves, either by reward for their suffering en route, or by riches for their toil once landed. Migrant stories are told like parables, with endings that tie up neatly, reaffirming our faith in mankind, or sounding a warning about what mankind is capable of.

These are one-dimensional images, told flat, heavily edited and primarily recounted from the host's perspective. That is the heart of this failure of humanization, that it is told from the host's perspective. It is spun to fit into a larger fabric, stitched in neatly, blending into the host society's values, agendas and even storytelling techniques. There is something grotesque about it sometimes, the sight of a migrant performing awkwardly to cameras, uncomfortable with the scrutiny but aware that it might bring help or relief, aware that they must condense their story into small resonant chunks. And when they are happy, they reflect the host society back to itself.

European media in particular are fixated on the binaries. The migrant is either a threat, collectively nouned as a 'swarm', or a benefit to the country. The latter is mostly in reaction to the former. It is understandable that in order to counter the ambient xenophobia in the rightwing media, that the migrant must be cast as exceptional, hardworking, tax-paying, a net good to the economy. There is even a sort of superhero migrant story favoured by some in the media; the French 'Spiderman' who scaled a tall building to save a child, the British Asian doctor who helped victims of the Manchester attack through the night, only to be subjected to racial abuse the next day, returning from his shift. I myself have fallen in the trap, writing in haste to defend and demonstrate the value of the migrant to the host country, but realized that in doing so I had validated the very premise that I was trying to refute – that a life had to be justified.

In London, there is a Syrian man who owns a falafel stand. He chants while selling his wares as he makes little falafel balls so quickly his fingers blur. 'Falafel falafel come get your falafel Syrian vegan and gluten free Tommy Robinson's best restaurant welcome welcome.' A woman films him and laughs, then posts it on social media. It turns out the man is a BAFTA winner, for a documentary about his precarious trip to the UK. He is described by the *Radio Times*

as today, every inch the modern Londoner. Leather bomber jacket, designer jeans and on-trend partially laced boots. Yet little more than two years ago, fleeing from Syria where he'd been imprisoned by President Assad's brutal regime, Hassan was in an overcrowded dinghy between Turkey and Greece fearing for his life as waves threatened to overwhelm the boat and tip him and 68 other desperate refugees into the sea. They were rescued by Turkish coastguards and he was able to complete the crossing the following day.

Here was a perfect sweet spot migrant protagonist, both successful and integrated, and a survivor of a treacherous journey.

But what of those not 'every inch the modern Londoner'? Those whose journeys did not take them over the seas and frozen roads of Europe, but through the banal and expensive bureaucracy of moving to a new country, the disruption of leaving a home from which you thought you would never move. Those whose new lives remain strange and unreal, who are reduced, in almost every way, as they try to learn a whole new world and language and way of being in no time at all. What of the ways every single day wounds them? New lives are not made organically, they are fashioned through the violence of small unfamiliarities. It is only because the migrant is 'other', that they are depicted in ways that highlight the route that brought them to a place, rather than the route once they get to a place. But intuitively, to make migrants feel welcome, or to incorporate them into the casual normality of life, it makes more sense to just show, rather than tell. I would watch a whole documentary about the tyranny of electronic checkout tills, the navigation of the recycling bins and rubbish collection days, the bewildering train system, the random moments of melancholy that pepper the life of a migrant, standing rain soaked in clothes not yet optimized, trying to figure out their way, to collect little pieces of Western city bark and straw, to nest in a hostile, unfamiliar environment.

In the world, nothing can be said to be certain but death and taxes, Benjamin Franklin wrote. But there is another certainty. People will move. They will move for necessity, for opportunity, for love, and on a whim. They will move between countries and within countries. Our very DNA is a product of people movement, mapped across races and continents. It is not only the most human story, it is *the* human story. Its essentializing, both positive and negative, into an exceptional phenomenon that is really a sort of cultural narcissism. It is also a fallout of the utter monopoly of the media by a certain reductive ideology and by a certain demographic, that which sees the story of a migrant and sells it to Lena Dunham. And it is a flattening that has accelerated because there is an inversely proportional relationship between the expansion of the entertainment complex and nuance. In the 1980s, the making of the British film *My Beautiful Launderette* from a screenplay by Hanif Kureishi seemed like a seminal moment, a work that finally told a story of migrants and their children with all its intensity and indignities, featuring thwarted parents, gay children and fascist friends. But in fact the opposite happened. It took another thirty years for another film to be made, Sathnam Sanghera's *The Boy with the Topknot*, which focused on mental health and cultural dislocation, for there to come another moment when a migrant experience could be told with nuance. Film makers and authors in the UK frequently complain that publishing houses and commissioning editors reject their pitches on the basis that they 'already' have a Muslim, black, or immigrant work in production, because there is clearly only one story to be told at a time.

The contrast with media organizations or independent documentary makers not based in large Western European or American cities and studios is illustrative. One of the most powerful accounts of the Syrian refugee crisis was that of a couple that was around 90 years old, andmarried for 65 years, who told their story as they joked, reminisced and wiped tears in their camp tent. It was made by a Turkish channel, TRT World, and managed in a few short minutes to encapsulate a lifetime of love, marriage, family, loss, and death.

There is no way forward other than handing the tools back to those from migrant backgrounds to do what they want with them. The narrative cannot be curated because the bases are loaded with expectation of a certain product – one which ends up inadvertently reifying all the dehumanizing stereotypes about migrants that it wishes to avoid.

Jade Jackman, *Calling Home*, 2017, 3.36 min.

Jade Jackman, *Calling Home*, 2017, 3.36 min.

I myself have fallen in the trap, writing in haste to defend and demonstrate the value of the migrant to the host country, but realized that in doing so I had validated the very premise that I was trying to refute—that a life had to be justified.

Nesrine Malik

I myself have fallen in the trap, writing in haste to defend and demonstrate the value of the migrant to the host country, but realized that in doing so I had validated the very premise that I was trying to refute—that a life had to be justified.

Nesrine Malik

I always say, 'We are over here because you were over there'; it's a very simple sentence.

Lubaina Himid

Lubaina Himid, *Negative Positives: The Guardian Archive, 2007–2017*

£1.60
Saturday 20.12.08
Published
in London and
Manchester
guardian.co.uk

theguardian
weekend edition

Gangs are getting younger and more violent, Met chief warns

Children killing each other over 'trivial' slights and girls increasingly involved

Christmas appeal Giving birth in Africa

Silence speaks louder than a flak-jacketed news hack

Anne Enright

A woman in Tiriri clinic lies on her side and labours in silence. It is early morning. Her husband, who sits beside her, looks worried, hopeful and forlorn. His wife's gaze has turned inwards, she is already in a different place. She doesn't seem frightened, as perhaps she should be. There is no pain relief here, and a week-old baby in the next room has just lost its mother to septicaemia.

I am astonished by the woman's silence. I am also worried that the look in her eyes seems so beautiful to me. Later I ask Brenda Acam, a student home from Kampala for the Christmas holidays, whether all the women of Katine give birth in silence. She laughs and says, 'You have children – did you not scream?' but yes, she agrees, 'Many of the women take their pain inside.'

It is the silences I find most disturbing in Katine. The children in the village are often hungry, but you do not hear that thin open cry of an unfed baby, or the outrage of a toddler surprised by the sudden emptiness of its belly. It seems

Continued on page 2 ▶

Sister Josephine Acen, centre, and her fellow traditional birth attendants in Katine Photograph: Dan Chung

Sandals
SAVE 25% + FREE NIGHTS

Haitian earthquake

Strong aftershock adds to chaos

Aid agencies call for urgent ban on adoptions

US will send 4,000 more troops to Port-au-Prince

Rory Carroll Port-au-Prince
Esther Addley

A new earthquake jolted Port-au-Prince yesterday, sending people fleeing on to the streets and complicating relief efforts as the US dispatched another 4,000 troops to Haiti.

A magnitude 5.9 quake, the most powerful aftershock since the 12 January cataclysm, rattled ruins in the capital and sowed panic but caused no serious reported damage or casualties.

Seismologists said the epicentre was about 35 miles south-west of the city and the focus was six miles deep. They warned of possible stronger aftershocks to come as the earth adjusted to new stresses caused by the original quake.

"Sometimes [they] die out very quickly. In other cases they can go on for weeks, or if we're really unlucky it could go on for months," Bruce Presgrave, of the US Geological Survey, told AP.

The dawn quake lasted about eight seconds, produced clouds of dust and sent people screaming from shelters. One woman with a heart condition died from fright. Others simply slept through it.

The government said it would send a response team to Petit-Goave, near the epicentre, where seven buildings reportedly collapsed. "We know they are going to need some help," said the prime minister, Jean-Max Bellerive.

Combined with drizzle which has compacted debris, the tremor compounded the multiple difficulties of teams seeing survivors and corpses buried amid semi-collapsed structures.

The quake killed an estimated 200,000 people, injured 250,000 and left 1.5 million homeless, according to the EU.

US dominance of the relief effort was likely to increase with a decision by the Pentagon to send another 2,000 US marines to Haiti, diverting troops that were on their way to the Gulf and Africa, to bolster the 12,000 already on the ground and on ships offshore.

Navy officials said yesterday that the three-ship USS Nassau amphibious ready group left port on Monday for its regular deployment but has been told to go Haiti instead for the earthquake relief effort.

The group is picking up marines in North Carolina and will include 2,000 sailors and 2,000 marines when it gets under way for Haiti, perhaps as early as today.

The first group of some 2,000 marines already off Haiti's shore went on land for the first time on Tuesday to help deliver aid. A Pentagon official says there are some 11,500 US military personnel in Haiti or offshore and 16,000 are expected by the end of the week. The first US Humvees were seen in Port-au-Prince on Tuesday.

Last week Hugo Chavez of Venezuela and Daniel Ortega of Nicaragua, both leftist presidents, accused Washington

of masking imperialism as aid. Haiti has welcomed the Americans but yesterday turned down an offer of 800 troops from the Dominican Republic, according to western diplomats because of historic tension between the neighbours.

A separate criticism of the international response came from aid agencies who called for an urgent moratorium on all adoptions from Haiti, saying that taking children out of the country at present risked causing long-term damage to already vulnerable children.

Thirteen agencies working together in the UK under the umbrella of the Disasters Emergency Committee said last night that many children apparently orphaned by the quake will have surviving relatives, and that efforts should instead be concentrated on reuniting families. Unicef and SOS Children, the world's largest orphan charity, also cautioned against hasty plans for large-scale adoption.

Miami's Catholic church has declared plans to fly hundreds of children to a new life in the US, while Edward Rendell, the governor of Pennsylvania, flew to Port-au-Prince to evacuate 54 orphans from the city after being told by Haiti's ambassador to the US that his presence could cut through red tape.

A party of Dutch social workers and immigration officials landed in Haiti earlier this week to evacuate 100 children whose adoptions were already under

Unicef cautioned against hasty adoptions. Agencies said efforts should be focused on reuniting families

way, while the US has waived visa requirements for Haitian children already going through the process and Canada is also fast-tracking adoptions.

Jasmine Whitbread, Save the Children's chief executive, said: "Taking children out of the country would permanently separate thousands of children from their families - a separation that would compound the acute trauma they are already suffering and inflict long-term damage on their chances of recovery."

Save the Children has teams in Haiti working on identifying lone children and tracing family members. World Vision's chief executive, Justin Byworth, said a wave of adoptions could leave children vulnerable to trafficking and abuse. Adoptions already in progress should go ahead, argued the agencies, as long as they conformed to local and international law.

Living conditions for survivors remained dire and though fewer bodies were visible the stench of death hung over Port-au-Prince.

Food, water and medical care seemed marginally more plentiful on Port-au-Prince's streets yesterday. "Supplies are beginning to get out to the people," the US defence secretary, Robert Gates, said during a visit to India. Banks are due to reopen shortly and some money transfer agencies are already functioning.

Seumas Milne, page 31 »

Looting horror Girl shot dead by police for taking paintings

Survivors

Numbers being pulled alive from ruins are testament to a resilient city

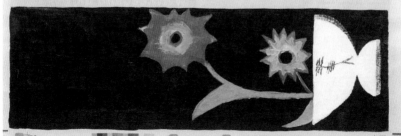

Lubaina Himid, *Negative Positives: The Guardian Archive, 2007–2017*

Negative Positives

— Lubaina Himid in Conversation with Ismail Einashe

Lubaina Himid is an artist and Professor of Contemporary Art at the University of Central Lancashire. Born in 1954 in Zanzibar, Himid was then raised in Britain where she became a pioneer of the Black Art movement, prominent in the 1980s. In 2010, she was appointed MBE for 'services to black women's art'. Himid's work has always eloquently addressed or uncovered issues relating to black identity and history, in Europe and the diaspora, but rose to a new prominence when she was awarded the 2017 Turner Prize. Here, Himid talks with Ismail Einashe about the aftermath of the Turner Prize, pressures that come with publicity, and the enduring need to address the colonial past in order to fully engage with the present.

Ismail Einashe How have things been since you won the Turner Prize in 2017? What has that recognition meant for you as a black female artist? You were, of course, prominently involved in the 1980s Black Art movement, but there are still not many black artists' voices.
— Lubaina Himid It is strange because I hear black artists' voices; I talk to artists of colour every day, because they're my friends and I've worked with them for years. How has it been? Well, since the day of the nomination, since that was announced, a lot of things changed extraordinarily. I'd never spoken to magazines, radio or TV to this extent ever. I am 63 now and I have been making the work and showing it publicly since I was

about 28. I live in a small city and since the announcement, wherever I am in the world, someone comes up to me and says, either 'Are you that person who was nominated for that thing?' or 'Are you Lubaina Himid who was nominated for the Turner Prize?' That kind of recognition has never happened to me before. I know it's only small – I'm not recognized on the streets of Rio de Janeiro – but in a local sense, it has meant that I've felt quite a lot of responsibility. In a community sense, in the community of black artists that I know, I felt an incredible pressure, not a pressure from them, but because I thought that I would be just another one in a long line of black women who have been nominated for the Turner Prize. I would be there for a bit of colour, something to pique interest, that kind of thing. I thought it must be a PR thing for the rule change because there was so much emphasis put on my age. [In 2017 the Prize's age restriction, that only artists under the age of 50 were eligible, was lifted.]

IE How did that make you feel?
—— LH Bad. I hadn't realized it would make me feel bad. I always knew how old I was, but I realized I really only had, say, twenty years of making, at most, left in my life. Sixty-three years had gone. Something really disconcertingly

pulled me up short; I was very aware, suddenly, of the shortness of life. There are constant questions about what it's like to be the oldest woman, and they are really bad. Generally speaking, people were incredibly supportive, and I've been able to have more conversations with people who I didn't think were that interested in art. I live in a bit of a sheltered world: I teach artists, my friends are artists, so in a way my everyday life is quite narrow. One thing I found is that a lot of people ask me to speak about politics. Of course, I know about politics like everyone else does, from what I read in the newspapers and see on the television, but I am not a politician or a community worker. Perhaps people think that it is easier to hear an artist talk about politics than someone who really knows. So, I have been refusing quite a lot of requests because I am not qualified to know the intricate and nuanced details of political situations in order to have an opinion.

IE What kind of requests are you getting?
—— LH Well, I get questions like, 'What do you think about international aid?' Of course, I think that it is complicated. I know it is a complicated question; I know that it is also very politicized, and decisions have gone into it. Or what do I think about the situation in Palestine?

I know what *I* think about it, I have an opinion, but only as I receive it, as everyone else receives it.

IE So suddenly, you become a spokesperson for everything that's black-related. Like, what do you think about the DRC [Democratic Republic of Congo]?
—— **LH** I don't know! And even if I do know, I'm not qualified to be an expert. Say a conference of textiles designers want me to give a keynote: I can add to that; I can talk about the politics of women's dress at a textile conference. But I feel incredible pressure when asked to talk like a politician. I can speak, you know. My gallerist said that I give good quote, [chuckles] but it's not the same as having an expertise in a subject and talking about it.

IE One of the things that is fascinating for me about your work is putting the spotlight on hidden histories of colonial slavery and other forms of black history in Europe and in the diaspora. I know that at the University of Central Lancashire you are working on the project called *Making Histories Visible*; why is it important to you and your work to tell those stories?
—— **LH** It's absolutely essential. I always say, 'We are over here because you were over there'; it's a very simple sentence. But this needs to be introduced early on in children's conversations, when you are saying, 'Here's a tree' or 'This is a dog'. Many other difficulties would be easier if there was a space for young people to think about how their everyday actions are related to the historical actions of their families. The fundamental idea of humans being equal needs to happen from the very beginning. It is a wilfully designed project not to. It is the same as suggesting that there have to be poor people for the system to work – we need to keep you people in poverty for everything to function. It's constructed; it isn't necessary and it is heartbreaking. The work itself seeks to point this out, show the gaps, give people agency and the ability to feel those gaps. It's never too late to have those conversations. *Making Histories Visible* is there to show young black artists the mistakes we made in the first place. We used to do shows called *Thin Black Line* or *Five Black Women*—they had to be called that because we were invisible, but by doing that we also boxed ourselves into a corner, and some artists found it difficult to get out of that box. On a personal level, I would always call myself a black woman artist, because it's important to me. I wanted to do that in the first place and I'm not changing now. But for other artists, talking about the spirituality of the work,

Lubaina Himid

131

the essence of the work is sometimes hampered by a constant narrative underneath that addresses race.

IE This morning you were saying that your work primarily is for black women. And that's been the backbone of your career from the very beginning. What is the importance of the work you do within communities to your work as a whole?
—— LH I make works so that the people who are actually trained to work with communities can work with the communities. I don't like this idea of artists working with communities. If they don't know what they're doing, they fly in from somewhere, link up with this black community, show them some stuff, then leave. The point is to work with the people who will be working with the community long after the exhibition has closed. It's also important to build what the people themselves have already brought, and that the museum has already has. So, I've been and gone, but I have given them something to start off the conversation.

IE You've spoken before about leaky borders, specifically in regard to your work in South Korea. It's not just about a physical border, it's also one of ideas. The imagery in your show reminds me a great deal of the leaky boats that cross the Mediterranean...
—— LH Yes, they are arranged in that wave formation to absolutely mirror the shape of that boat, to remind you of the boatyard. There is a gap between each of those planks, and the point is that the only thing that can fill it is you. You can go inside it, but you can see through it. Some of it is to recreate Korean boats, the way of defending the Korean borders against the Japanese, against the Chinese. I made this thing in 2014. Three times in my life there have been these big boat stories. When I was much younger there were the Vietnamese boat people who were treated in a completely different way, and then the Cuban boat people, and then the African boat people. But, yes, the fragility of boats and also their construction; these are people carriers, that's what boats are. They're in a sense the most ludicrous people carriers if you consider the dangers of the sea. Who the hell thought that a boat was adequate for such a space? It's like going into outer space in a shoebox. Dangerous, and fragile.

IE Another thing that struck me is the way your work addresses the leakiness or the fragility of the past and the present. As a black journalist working across Europe, I feel the historical legacy of slavery, of

132

colonialism in the present in very real ways.

—— **LH** The past is always present in the room with us, and we can be present in the future. The present is a fluid place. Absolutely, definitely. We don't exist at all in this sort of bubble of today. But there is a tendency in European conversation to try to box in the present. Brexit is a prime example of not thinking about future consequences, and not understanding the past; not seeing the present, in a very positive way, as a rich mixture of the past and the future. It is just such an obvious way of thinking.

You can't have a decent conversation about food without referring to the colonial past, or clothes, everyday things. Never mind the more serious conversations about how we live. I think the collective amnesia in mainland Europe is astonishing. It actually makes the British look utterly radical and forward-thinking. I think the British have sorted it in a much better way certainly than, as far as I know, the French, the Italians, the Dutch, and the Germans. People cannot and will not make those connections. Part of having shows in Europe is so that I can say to curators: 'Yes, I'd love to have a show here. But one of the things I'd like to do is to have an external programme in which you ask artists who are black who work here in this country to talk about their work.' So, as part of this show, Christine Eyene, who works with me at Central Lancashire but who is also the director of the Biennial of Casablanca, is speaking to the curator about black artists that they know working in France at this time. Some of those artists are French citizens, and some have come from other places. It was very, very important to me to have this discussion in French, so that it was accessible – also to people who perhaps had come from somewhere else, and whose first language was something else, but who spoke French.

IE I want to ask you about your work *Negative Positives*. Why is it important to challenge how people of colour are framed in the media?

—— **LH** Because you see it every day. Black people are presented again, and again, and again in a similar way in newspapers, and that way has almost nothing to do with how we encounter each other or how white people encounter black people in the everyday. White people don't encounter black people in Britain armed to the teeth with knives and guns; we all encounter each other in shops and offices and in parks and listening to music or whatever. Yet we are rarely presented in this public way. For example, showing a football

Lubaina Himid

133

or rugby player posed next to a waste container. You might say that's an everyday image, but it is sending a message, a message that is very clear to me, that this man is only worth standing next to something that is rotting and stinking. You would never see a white cricket player leaning against such a container, and very often you won't see a black man leaning against a tree – or if you did there would be other stories there, too. It's not that easy to undo the histories of art or photography, because they are strong. Photography has always been used as a way of accusing criminals and documenting the evidence of wrongdoing; probably the greatest number of photographs of black people are where they have been arrested and photographed. There's another image I have to mention; it isn't in this collection. Following a earthquake in Haiti, which caused widespread destruction, the *Guardian* took a photo of a black woman lying on the ground with blood coming out of her head, and next to her is a painting. The small caption reads that she had stolen the painting and been shot. She was a looter, you know. So, OK, she stole a painting – big deal! [chuckles] – and hooray, the thing she wanted to take was a painting! And she was shot. And the *Guardian* wanted to show this. But never, never, never have I seen a dead white woman lying on the ground with blood coming out of her head. That to me is the image. It doesn't matter to me whether I am picking out the subtleties and nuances of these negative positive things. That image for me will always say this newspaper doesn't care enough.

Lubaina Himid, *Negative Positives: The Guardian Archive, 2007–2017*

Football

Drogba ready to stay at Chelsea at least this season

Focus now on winning trophies with Blues

Club deny Van Basten link with manager's job

David Hytner

Didier Drogba would consider a reunion with Jose Mourinho when the former Chelsea manager resurfaces at his next club, but the striker's immediate focus is on staying at Stamford Bridge for the rest of the season and winning major honours.

The Ivory Coast international, who has recently been kept out of the team by a knee injury, was angry and disappointed when Mourinho vacated his position at the club last week and was replaced by Avram Grant, the Israeli who was brought in as the director of football in the summer.

Drogba was not the only player to have felt let down. Other senior squad members, most notably Frank Lampard, the England midfielder, credit Mourinho with making them the players they are, and there has been incredibly that the club's most successful manager was allowed to leave.

Yet the tears have now dried up and been replaced by pragmatism. Grant lacks the charisma of Mourinho and there are those in the squad who believe he was attracted — an assertion the club have been moved to deny.

But with crucial games on the horizon, not least in the Champions League, Drogba and his team-mates have resolved to focus on getting the results that would raise morale. Nothing can bring back Mourinho; Grant is the man for whom they must play.

Grant had little time to prepare the team for last Sunday's Premier League defeat at Manchester United, having only been given the job on the Thursday, but he and the players enjoyed themselves more at a Hull City on Wednesday night, where they recorded a 4-0 Carling Cup victory.

"Things have been difficult of late but

we managed to pick ourselves up," said John Terry, the captain. "We will do our best to maintain the team spirit throughout Chelsea. Manchester United was a very tough game but [beating Hull] is the right result just before the weekend game [at home to Fulham].

"It was a great win and certainly well needed as we hadn't won in four games. Hull is a tough place to come but we played well and scored goals which we had not been doing. We knew they would get in our faces for the first 15 minutes but we matched them and then our football did the talking."

Certain players believe they could well outlast Grant but the club have been keen to stress that the incumbent has their full support. Tongues were set wagging by the presence of Marco van Basten in the Old Trafford directors' box but the Holland manager insisted he attended only to talk with Edwin van der Sar, his goalkeeper and captain, an arrangement which had been made some weeks previously.

"Chelsea Football Club totally refute that the job of manager at first-team coach has been offered to any individual other than Avram Grant," the club said in a statement.

> 'You have to accept that Drogba is 29 turning 30 and that needs to be taken into consideration'

Drogba is receptive to the idea of playing under Mourinho again and were the Portuguese to take another job before the end of January and the closure of the winter transfer window, Drogba could have a decision to make. But he will not quit Chelsea lightly or on a whim.

Drogba has spoken in the past of wanting to experience another European culture. Having sampled those of France and England, he would be tempted by Italy or Spain, where Real Madrid would like to sign him, despite voicing concern about his age. "Totally independent of his situation with Chelsea, you have to accept that he's 29 turning 30 and that needs to be taken into consideration for us," said Pini Drag Mijatovic, Real's sporting director.

Grant had one worry lifted yesterday, with Uefa set to allow him to coach his players from the touchline in next Wednesday's Champions League tie against Valencia at the Mestalla stadium without a Pro Licence.

Uefa rules state that coaches in the Champions League need the licence to enter the technical area but the European governing body will permit Grant to fulfil his duties without restraint during the 12-week period of grace allowed by the Premier League while the issue over his lack of a licence is resolved.

Grant has the highest form of coaching badge that was available when he qualified in Israel. He may be asked to sit a refresher course to obtain the new qualification.

Blues' big deals

When the contracts run out for the biggest stars at Stamford Bridge

Petr Cech Summer 2010	Didier Drogba Summer 2010
John Terry Summer 2012	Michael Essien Summer 2012
Ricardo Carvalho Summer 2012	Michael Ballack Summer 2009
Frank Lampard Summer 2009	A Shevchenko Summer 2010

Didier Drogba has his eyes on winning trophies at Stamford Bridge despite feeling let down by the departure of Jose Mourinho from Chelsea Tom Hevezi/AP

Blues vow to fight charges of losing control

David Hytner

Chelsea have declared they will defend themselves "strongly" against two Football Association charges relating to the conduct of their players and the assistant coach, Steve Clarke, that arose from the 2-0 Premier League defeat at Manchester United last Sunday.

The club instead accused of failing to control their players — for the fourth time in 18 months — while Clarke has been charged with using foul and/or insulting behaviour to match officials after the game.

The first flashpoint followed the referee Mike Dean's decision to send off Mikel John Obi, the Chelsea midfielder, for his two-footed tackle on United's Patrice Evra. At least four Chelsea players crowded around Dean, including the captain John Terry, and the referee felt sufficiently intimidated and concerned to include the incident in his match report.

Terry attempted to snatch the red card from Dean's hand but because the referee saw the incident and elected not to pass censure there and then, the FA had no recourse to retrospective action against the defender. They would not have relished charging the England captain.

Chelsea's new manager, Avram Grant, complained that three key decisions went against his team — the sending-off, the fact that United's opening goal came after 2½ minutes of first-half stoppage time had been played and the awarding of a dubious late penalty for the second goal. Clarke voiced the perceived injustices with more venom when he encountered the officials in the tunnel.

"Chelsea Football Club will be strongly defending the two charges issued by the Football Association and will be considering that defence until we have to respond on October 12," said a club statement.

The charge against the club is not believed to be at the most severe end of the spectrum but it is the latest of a series. In April 2006, Chelsea were fined £10,000 for failing to control their players after they surrounded the referee Mark Halsey against West Brom. A month later they were given a further £10,000 fine and warned as to their future conduct by an FA disciplinary commission after being found guilty of the same charge during the 1-0 league defeat at Fulham. They had pleaded not guilty. And last season, they received a £100,000 fine and a reprimand for their part in the brawl with Arsenal players during the Carling Cup final.

John Terry argues with the referee Mike Dean as Mikel John Obi sees red

Lubaina Himid, Negative Positives: The Guardian Archive, 2007–2017

Three times in my life there have been these big boat stories. When I was much younger there were the Vietnamese boat people who were treated in a completely different way, and then the Cuban boat people, and then the African boat people.

Lubaina Himid

The thin line between
the real and unreal:
My sea is imaginary, unlike
the fluid graveyard of the
Mediterranean. My boat is
only for one, not crowded
like the ones filled with
terrified children. We all
float, they and I, through the
indignation, the shame, the
bleakness... And to all of us
it feels the same: Absurd.

Ece Temelkuran

The thin line between
the real and unreal:
My sea is imaginary, unlike
the fluid graveyard of the
Mediterranean. My boat is
only for one, not crowded
like the ones filled with
terrified children. We all
float, they and I, through the
indignation, the shame, the
bleakness... And to all of us
it feels the same: Absurd.

Ece Temelkuran

Roda Abdalle, *Avskild, (Decluded)*, 2017, 3.00 min.

Roda Abdalle, Avskild, (Decluded), 2017, 3.00 min.

The Paper Pain

— Ece Temelkuran

Across the level ocean of her mind come floating certain refugees in a makeshift plastic boat so crowded with passengers they are stacked in layers and dropping over the sides. She has seen this picture. She has read that larger ships might sail very near, that they might stop to consider the woe and the odds, then keep going. Sometimes bottles of water or biscuits were tossed from the larger ships before they started their engines again. What could she put against the desolation of that moment, watching the ship start its engines again. What is the price of desolation, and who pays. Some questions don't warrant a question mark.
Ann Carson, '1 = 1', *The New Yorker*, 11 January 2016

Over the last two years I have become my own home. And recently I gave up the toil of trying to remember what has really happened. Since then, my reference has been my own memory. What I remember, although it sometimes truly is unreal, cannot be refuted. Some call this 'lonely'; I call it 'being on my own'. It started when I began to live on the border that my writing has been inhabiting for decades; the thin line that supposedly separates fiction from non-fiction, the line that *flows* between the real and whatever its opposite is considered to be. Therefore, I swim in an ocean of fears and fantasies – that is what imagination is when you are on your own. I am what I imagine myself now to be. I am what I write. A blurry ocean of

the things that happen, the things that might not have happened
and things that have not happened.

At home I have a table that I put together myself, bought from the
Ikea in Zagreb, in 2016, after the putsch in Turkey and before political and
moral insanity took over the entire country, alongside irreversible damage
to the human condition. There is a laptop on the table the keys of which
I keep pounding and a notebook with black pages that I write on with white
ink. Despite the fact that I write other stories about other people on this
table, people continue to call me 'the exile'.

The unreal: I named the table Kon-Tiki. Too weak a boat to cross the
ocean of international politics and finally find a shore that I can call home,
but solid enough to keep rowing in. Since the day I built Kon-Tiki, I have
written articles in English for the papers you read. About truth – mine and
yours – and about politics – mostly yours.

The thin line between the real and unreal: My sea is imaginary, unlike
the fluid graveyard of the Mediterranean. My boat is only for one, not
crowded like the ones filled with terrified children. We all float, they and I,
through the indignation, the shame, the bleakness... And to all of us it feels
the same: Absurd. 'Is this my life now?' 'Is this happening to me?'
So, we row.

'EXILED' says the giant screen behind me. My name is there, next to it, for
some three thousand people to see. I am on stage, at the Lincoln Center,
in New York, and I am sitting next to Hillary Clinton, of all people. This is
real, it is 2018. What feels unreal is that word, 'exiled', next to my name.
I had never said it, but it kept appearing next to my name. Did I forget to
tell the organization that I don't want that word to define me? Didn't I tell
them, half-jokingly, as I have done at similar events for the last two years
that 'exile' has apparently become the sexiest word in my biography,
overshadowing all the other things that I manage to do?

I stop the event, which is supposed to be about rising right-wing
populism across the world, and start talking about that giant word behind
me, 'exiled'. 'Why do they hardly mention the names of the Syrian refugees
on TV? How many of us believe that bread, a blanket, and clean water
would suffice for the survival of human dignity? Not theirs, but the dignity
of Europeans. And there are those idiots who believe that if they call them
immigrants on the news enough times the boat people will turn from refugees to people who can be deported. Shame is a scarce commodity. Why
is it so hard to name their names when they crave it, and why is it so easy

to name me the 'exile' when I reject that term? Why do you rescue *me* but not them? Why are you so enthusiastic about me, yet reluctant when it comes to them?'

This is not real. I did not say these words. But I wouldn't dare to call it unreal. Would you?

The reality: I talked to them, the audience, about their victimhood, as opposed to my assumed suffering. I told them they too would feel like an exile, a refugee in their own country once the political and moral insanity takes over their land as it did mine. And that the words 'exile' or 'refugee' do not require someone to change location in today's world – those who are capable of critical thinking will all feel homeless soon.

Or did I tell this to another audience in America? When travelling alone one loses the references of time and space. When drifting in the night the boat loses the point of triangulation.

'On several media outlets we see that you have been called an exile? Are you an exile?' This is a Turkish journalist now. Asking me about the word that I didn't choose to live with. 'Western mainstream intellectual circles and the media have a certain romanticism towards women like me, women of letters. Probably their distorted and embellished perception has its roots in the mythological image of Europa, saved from the bull. I am now the lady saved from the horrors of the tyrant, the Scheherazade rescued from the hands of the barbarian. This construction automatically bestows upon them gallantry, knighthood. My assumed identity as an exile in a Western land turns them into the prince who saves the damsel in distress. How convenient. How cleansing. Not for me, for them. What is most annoying to me is that I have to stick to the role. You are not supposed to talk about anything other than your victimhood, and certainly should not cease to play the damsel in distress. How exhausting. How unsustainable.'

This is real. Entirely.

Here is something unreal:

Dear Ann Carson,
You know very well that 1 is not equal to 1. Because I am certain that you know the one and more importantly you know about the other one. I am the one. And the woman in that crowded boat with a life jacket, the one who stares at the real ocean of indignity that lies before her is the other one. We are not equal; at least that is what the world tends to believe. Therefore, most probably you know the

price of desolation and who pays for it. You: the one who is able to see the desolation, that nameless woman in the boat who is suffering, and me: the one with a name that weighs too heavily as I row.
Do you think there was desolation before the word desolation was invented? I am never sure of these things.
Yours faithfully, Ece (not the EXILE)

The privilege of words, the ability to articulate and the opportunity of being published allow my desolation to solidify – as opposed to any other woman literally crossing the literal sea. My pain is deciphered and therefore human. She, on the other hand is a muted creature; easier to misinterpret and, finally, dehumanize. Although I know it is the same pain we suffer; the irritating feeling that something is missing, that something is missing all the time especially when you are supposed to be content. It feels like the sleep a child sleeps in a car that is approaching home, knowing that no one will carry her in their arms to bed. That half-awake uneasiness that keeps scratching the warm tenderness of sleep.

My abstraction is more present than their reality, the ones on the boat, just as Anna Karenina is more present than any living woman has been or will be. They will have to wait to tell tales of their sorrow until a grandchild is born to listen, just as the survivors of all tragedy have done throughout human history. Pain skips a generation to be learned. I don't have to wait. My story in fact cannot wait. It has to be served to the media, to the audiences now, while it is fresh. When the story of my country falls from the headlines to the third page, I will disappear. They will expect me to disappear. Another woman suffering in another language, 'the tragedy of the month' will occupy the stage then. She will present sentences with a different syntax to explain that she is more than an exile, that she is a person with a longer story. 'Life is a bigger journey', she will say. 'And what you call "exile" is only a part of it.' Mine and hers is a boat that is forced to drop anchor in a particular point in time, expected to stay still, unlike other, real boats that are expected to move and keep moving to another shore.

As for the question of who pays for the desolation, I mean, if you want the reality, mostly they calculate the price according to the number of words. The silent get nothing, naturally.

Being branded as an 'exile' is a geographic domain where you can talk to the living yet prefer to converse with the dead. A *mare clausum*, a closed sea, so to speak, where the dead ones of my ilk understand who I am better than the living. One of the souls buried in this fluid graveyard is Joseph Brodsky. He truly was a crazy person. Do you know the story about him? Before he fled the former USSR and long before he became the Nobel Laureate, he was sent to a labour camp. The prisoners were supposed to cut wood for a certain period of time every day. Once Brodsky started, however, he did not stop. It is said that he cut wood for ten hours before the guards forced him to stop. From then on, he was never forced to cut wood. The prison decided not to raise the bet. He must have been like Rosa Luxembourg who applied to herself a stricter discipline than her prison's regulations in order to feel like she could seize control of her time and her existence. Years later, in *Grief and Reason: Essays* (1995) Brodsky wrote (in English) that he was no different from other ordinary refugees and rejected being placed in the more privileged level of homelessness, that of the exiled writer/poet. Once again, he drew the borders of his existence but this time he probably learned that it isn't as easy as cutting the wood for ten hours. You can escape prison by building your own prison, and you can escape the word prisoner by terrifying the guards, but protecting your-self against the word 'exile' is another story. The word sounds so compas-sionate that it makes your rejection look like an interesting yet unnecessary rebellion. The word is so accommodating that only a few understand why you are trying to burn such a shelter located in the neighbourhood of the privileged – especially when you are homeless. Brodsky never wrote the sentence but he could have; in my *mare clausum*, when I speak to him he repeats the sentence 'I am my own home. I became my home.'

Hannah Arendt is another soul I frequent whenever I am made to struggle with the word 'exile'. She spoke and wrote about the audience that expected her to talk about herself, her victimhood. She tried to joke when-ever she spoke, a tactic that always causes uneasiness for audiences because it violates the limits of the 'lady in distress' act. The word 'exile' expects you to carry a face that has forgotten how to laugh. She was at home though as long as she wrote, at home with her mischievous laughter. She was her own home too.

Simone Weil, Breyten Breytenbach, who was called 'exile' at the same age that I was, Julio Cortázar, and many others have fought with the word and resisted the perceptions of audiences that made them lonelier than they actually were. The word put them in a separate place where silent refugees aren't permitted.

How can I explain all this in a TV or radio sound-bite? I hear Hannah

147

Arendt in a rare TV interview, saying with her silences, 'How primitive these questions about the condition of the exile are! How stupid.' Maybe the next woman who will be branded as an exile, who will replace me on this stage where one is expected not to laugh, will hear the same in my silences as well. And I will whisper to her, 'I am my home. Aren't you? Well you will be. You will be very soon.'

In this unreal sea, this sea where I frequently lose my bearings, the sea that might easily swallow my Kon-Tiki, *the real* hits me at seemingly irrelevant, certainly insignificant and always unexpected times. For example, at a hair-dresser in Zagreb. The worst thing that can happen to a person with curly hair is to need a haircut in Europe where curly hair is always a deviation, impossible to untangle. My hair should be cut when it is dry because there is a different mathematics to curly hair (it's a long and boring story). So, here I am, trying to explain to the over-confident hairdresser the algorithms of cutting curly hair. He does not give the tiniest shit. I feel like an alien; I am an alien. And now I am an alien with curly hair. The prolonged conver-sation begins to embarrass me and to the audience in the hairdresser I start looking like a mad woman obsessed with her hair. All the eyes, those blank stares shrink me to a helpless soul. I am scaled down to reality, a refugee. It is not like being on stage where I can articulate my rejection of their branding of me and sound human. I am mute now. Like the woman on the boat, I am rowing and rowing *across the level ocean of my mind.* So, for a long time I have been cutting my own hair.

'I have a longer story', I whisper. 'I am a human.' I am not *the* one. I am one. And the difference between those two claims is more than about 'the'. It is about a damn lifetime. And one always – both on land and on sea – is equal to one.

Roda Abdalle, *Avskild, (Decluded)*, 2017, 3.00 min.

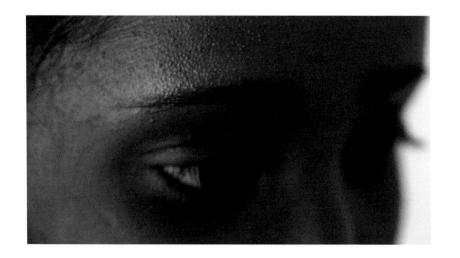

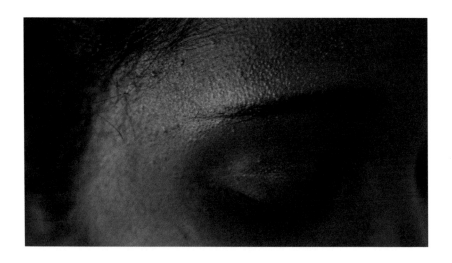

Roda Abdalle, *Avskild, (Decluded)*, 2017, 3.00 min.

What feels unreal is that word, "exiled", next to my name. I had never said it, but it kept appearing next to my name.

Ece Temelkuran

What feels unreal is that word, "exiled", next to my name. I had never said it, but it kept appearing next to my name.

Ece Temelkuran

Displaced in Media 2017–2019

— Menno Weijs

As a response to the media framing of the 'refugee crisis', the European Cultural Foundation (ECF) brought over thirty journalists, activists, and people working in the field of journalism and media literacy from across the continent to Amsterdam in the spring of 2017. This was the beginning of the 'Displaced in Media' strategic partnership – a pan-European group that would work together over the coming years to find ways to reclaim media narratives on migration and migrants in Europe. During that first enlightening and invigorating week, this group engaged in discussions, workshops, and public events, in order not only to expose the flaws in the ways that the media cover migration, but also to imagine new collaborative, cross-border, and diverse methodologies to challenge the media, and to give the stage to content by migrants.

The first proposition that the group made was that even though migrants had arrived in Europe, they had not yet entered the public sphere. The few times that they did, they were presented as characters in other people's stories, as desperate faces, surging hordes and dead bodies; we rarely ever hear from migrants themselves. The Displaced in Media project aimed to address this disjuncture by challenging media orthodoxies and to provide a stage for migrants to tell their own stories.

The project aimed to support the numerous journalists, filmmakers, cultural professionals, activists, and researchers who are trying to break through the traditional mainstream media in their local contexts, and who are engaged in media activism that promotes marginalized voices. These organizations and individuals have paved the way for the production of media that are fair and that do not seek to frame migrants through a problematizing lens. These include migrant-led media initiatives as well as institutions grappling with the same issues.

Thus, the Displaced in Media strategic partnership was formed of nine organizations from eight European countries. While the European Cultural Foundation convened the group, it was very much a collaboration led by our partners, all of whom were organizations that do urgent, vital work in media literacy and journalism. They included ZEMOS98 (Seville), Association of Creative Initiatives "ę" (Warsaw), the British Film Institute (London), MODE Istanbul, Les Têtes de l'Art (Marseille), Fanzingo (Botkyrka), Kurziv (Zagreb) and Here to Support (Amsterdam).

Following that first Amsterdam event, the Displaced in Media project began in earnest. Further events were held across Europe: from Seville to Marseilles to London. Each event tried to better facilitate the project's overall cross-border European collaboration on media literacy and journalism through facilitating the exchange of knowledge and methodologies, as well as fostering the inclusion of migrant perspectives in the countries of each member organization. Taken together, it was hoped these workshops would contribute to fostering broader shifts in the European public sphere. What emerged was a unique community of practice; one that is gradually creating an infrastructure for underrepresented perspectives to be heard. This process brought into the world a cross-European network of peers in journalism and media literacy who are keen to pool their knowledge and educational methodologies, as well as create strategies for that network to reach general audiences through mainstream media, and engage in dialogue with policy makers.

The two-year-long project produced a series of tangible outcomes: an online resource – the Displaced in Media Lab; a book of practical suggestions for media makers, styled as a Recipe Book; a policy paper aimed at policy makers. Perhaps most significantly, the project produced a number of media works made by young refugees and migrants working with the partner organizations. One such video, made by Mulham Mohamed Hidel, a Palestinian-Syrian vlogger living in Istanbul, captures the project's overall aims in a nutshell. Hidel, walking through the parks by Istanbul's ancient city walls turns to the camera and asks, with a smile, 'why are people looking at me?'. Of course, it is obvious why people are looking at him:

he is walking through the city while talking to a selfie stick. But we are with him – he is choosing one audience, elbowing away another, and taking his place in physical and digital public space. The video was produced at a video-making workshop run by Small Projects Istanbul, a small NGO that works with young people.

Other initiatives developed methods for encouraging people with less natural inclination to speak out to have a voice. In Marseille – a city shaped by centuries of migrations and reactions to them – the community arts organizations Les Têtes de l'Art and Boulègue TV worked with young refugees to make 'audio-visual postcards'. Refugees created scripts by writing letters to friends and then cutting them with footage filmed on their phones. The results sit somewhere between activism, therapy, and art. In his film, one refugee, called Mory, writes a letter to his friend about the horrors that await him if he attempts to come to Europe. 'Think of your mother and sisters before you sacrifice yourself', he warns.

Fanzingo is a youth organization that supports young people's art. It is based in Botkytra, a suburb of Stockholm where 65 percent of the population was born outside of Sweden. Every Wednesday evening they hold an open-door session for local youths who are interested in making films. Young people come with their ideas for films, and Fanzingo youth workers help to produce them. In the past year this 'medialab' has produced two short films, which are currently being shown at film festivals across Europe; a women's group for newcomers to share experiences; and a video series sharing the perspectives of first-time voters, which was broadcast on national TV. In the short film she made with the 'medialab', titled, *I'm Tired*, Sara El Kelany and another Fanzingo participant express the exhausting sensation of living with the threat of deportation.

Some projects within the network are more concerned with using media to directly address structural prejudice. Creative Initiatives "ę" is a Warsaw-based socially engaged arts organization with a network of community workers across Poland. They worked in Przemyśl, a town in southern Poland where young Poles and Ukrainians are not only educated separately, but lead segregated lives. They made a film series with young-sters from both communities to start a conversation in school about differ-ence and prejudice. In Spain, community media organization ZEMOS98 ran a series of workshops with anti-racist organization SOS Racismo, looking at ways of countering Islamophobia on Twitter. We Are Here, a migrant squatter movement in Amsterdam, occupies buildings to provide shelter for people struggling with the asylum system – what they call being 'in

Menno Weijs

limbo'. They are working on a media platform that syndicates DIY videos and vlogs made by people in refugee collectives across Europe. In his video, Eric Bimule, a member of the We Are Here collective, protests against forced deportations outside the Ministry of Justice and Security in The Hague. A year after the encounter in Amsterdam, another thirty contributors to the Displaced in Media project met in Seville to finalize the Recipe Book, outline an advocacy strategy and contribute to the development of MediActivism.eu, the platform that collects all the media produced by the project.

The final element of the infrastructure was related to advocacy. If we want newcomers to become participants in, rather than subjects of, public debate, we need to address the systemic mechanisms that facilitate exclusion and marginalization. Such mechanisms are anchored in policy, from the very local to the European level, and also in the way media organizations function. In our policy publication – and at a Policy Forum in Marseille – we presented the practices and learnings of Displaced in Media to policy makers.

As a whole, the Displaced in Media project demonstrates the extent to which audio-visual languages are powerful tools for social transformation. However, the media environment is so loaded that helping content find its way into the mainstream is a complex challenge. The community of practice has set itself the goal of establishing relations with major newspapers and radio and TV channels across Europe. At an event at the British Film Institute in London we established such connections with mainstream media and professionals active in media education.

Displaced in Media doesn't end here. The channels of collaboration, the bolstered discourse, and our contributions to a transformative process are all part of a new infrastructure that has been constructed by the strategic partnership. This infrastructure will continue to be used by initiatives and collectives working towards the transformation of media and policy across Europe, part of which is represented by this volume, *Lost in Media*.

If you want to know more about the process from which this publication, *Lost in Media*, evolved, we invite you to read the *Displaced in Media Recipe Book*, the *Displaced in Media Magazine* and watch the films on MediActivism.eu. Please do so, and you will see that the contributors should no longer be reduced to the singular identity of 'refugee'. They are no longer just subjects of public debate, but citizens who have claimed their space in the public sphere.

Menno Weijs

In compiling the various strands of *Lost in Media,* we wanted to include visual content that did more than merely illustrate the arguments of our contributors. To that end we brought together a number of different artists and filmmakers – some well-known, some less so – to help anchor some of the themes of the book. In so doing we relied on films produced by young filmmakers of a migrant or refugee background as well as the work of more prominent artists, each responding to the core themes of displacement.

The four films we chose by young filmmakers of a migrant or refugee background come from the Displaced in Media programme (discussed by Menno Weijs on pages 153-156). In his short film *The Most Racist Advertisements in History,* the journalist Moha Gerehou (also an author in this volume), reflects on the way mainstream media have created a stereo-typical image of black people through history and how this can be hacked in order to introduce new narratives and ways of turning our backs to these racist contents. In *It's Not Hard,* Mulham Mohamed Hidel, a young Syrian migrant in Istanbul, walks the city's ancient walls, discussing his loss of friends and community and his need to discover purpose in life. *Anonim* is an anonymous work made by filmmakers in Poland that explores tensions between the Ukrainian and Polish populations in the country. Jade Jackman's film *Calling Home,* documents the reality of female asylum seekers in the Yarls Wood detention centre through the recordings of phone calls. Finally, Roda Abdalle's film *Avskild,* a film about the emotional experience of displacement in Sweden. (All the films from Displaced in Media can be found at MediActivism.eu)

Elsewhere, Jillian Edelstein's photographic series *Life Seekers* consti-tutes a unique perspective on Lesvos, one of the most iconic flashpoints of the 'migrant crisis'. The work of Jacob Lawrence, too, was important for us to include. Lawrence's *Migration Series* of 1941 tells of a different move-ment of people – the Great Migration of African Americans to the northern United States from the South that began in the 1910s – yet it echoes many of the universal themes of this book. Finally, we include the work of the two artists we were lucky to interview in this volume, Tania Bruguera and Lubiana Himid, both of whom, in very different ways, pinpoint in their work the tensions and contradictions within the mediatised representation of migrant and refugee bodies.

Finally, the inside back and front cover uses an image by the mayor of Liverpool, Joe Anderson, of the artist Banu Cennetoğlu's work *The List.*

The work is a text-based installation of names of migrants killed making the crossing to Europe; it was defaced when it was installed as part of the 2018 Liverpool Biennale. Anderson's image, which was posted to Twitter, has come to represent the tensions that culture has been invested with in the years since the 'migrant crisis'.

ABOUT THE CONTRIBUTORS

Tania Bruguera (b.1968) is a Cuban installation and performance artist. She lives and works in both New York and Havana, and has participated in numerous international exhibitions. Her work is also in the permanent collections of many institutions, including the Museum of Modern Art and Bronx Museum of the Arts and the Museo Nacional de Bellas Artes de La Habana. Bruguera's work pivots around issues of power and control, and several of her works interrogate and re-present events in Cuban history. As part of the work, Bruguera has launched an Immigrant Respect Awareness Campaign and launched an international day of action on 18 December 2011 (which the UN has designated International Migrants Day), in which other artists will also make work about migration.

Ismail Einashe (b.1984) is a journalist and writer. He studied Social Sciences at the University of Cambridge and Politics at the University of London. Einashe has written for the *Guardian*, *The Sunday Times*, *Frieze*, *The Nation*, *NPR* and *The New York Times*, among many other publications. He is on the editorial board of the *Tate Etc.*, the magazine of the Tate Museums. He has worked for *BBC Radio Current Affairs* and as a presenter on BBC Radio. Einashe has reported from over a dozen countries across Europe, Africa, and the Middle East, covering everything from migration and refugee issues to human rights and conflict. He is a 2019 Alicia Patterson Foundation Fellow, a Dart Center Ochberg Fellow at Columbia University Journalism School and an associate at The Centre for the Study of Global Human Movement at the University of Cambridge. Einashe lives and works between Nairobi, Addis Ababa and London.

Moha Gerehou (b.1992 in Huesca, Spain, with roots from Gambia) is a journalist at eldiario.es and an activist at Federación SOS Racismo in Spain. He works in a number of areas related to anti-racism, with a special focus on the media. His works, through articles and videos, are published in various magazines and online. He also has developed 'If I were a black character in a movie', a show about the representation of black people in films, TV series, advertisements and photography.

Aleksandar Hemon (b.1964, Sarajevo) is the author of many books, including *The Lazarus Project,* which was a finalist for the National Book Critics Circle Award and the National Book Award, and of a couple of non-fiction books: *My Parents: An Introduction* and *This Does Not Belong to You* and , forthcoming in June 2019. Hemon has worked as a writer for Radio Sarajevo Youth Programmne, and then as a waiter, canvasser, bookseller, bike messenger, as a supervisor at a literacy centre and as teacher of English as a second language (all in Chicago). His work has been featured in many prestigious publications such as *The New Yorker*, *Esquire*, *Granta* and *The New York Times*. He has written for film and television, most recently for the Netflix show *Sense8*. He has been the recipient of a Guggenheim Fellowship, a 'genius grant' from the MacArthur Foundation, and many other awards. He has taught at several universities in the US before finally settling at Princeton University.

Lubaina Himid (b.1954, Zanzibar) is a British painter who has dedicated her 30-year-long career to uncovering marginalized and silenced histories, figures, and cultural moments. Himid currently lives and works in Preston, UK, where she is Professor of Contemporary Art at the University of Central Lancashire. She is the 2017 winner of the Turner Prize, and was awarded a MBE in 2010 and CBE in 2018 for her services to art. She has exhibited at numerous institutions and international exhibitions, including Tate Britain, London. She has forthcoming solo exhibitions in 2019 at the New Museum, New York; Frans Hals Museum, Haarlem; and Tate Britain, London. Her work is represented in significant public collections, including Tate, Arts Council England, and the UK Government Art Collection.

Dawid Krawczyk (b. 1991) is a journalist. He studied Philosophy and English Philology at the University of Wrocław. He writes reportages, feature stories, and reviews. His works are regularly published in *Krytyka Polityczna* (Political Critique) and *Gazeta Wyborcza*. In recent years he has focused mainly on international drug policy, migration, and Polish politics. His articles have been published in Polish, English, Czech, Hungarian, Romanian, and Italian. Krawczyk lives and works in Warsaw, Poland.

Antonija Letinić (b. 1979) studied art history and French language and literature at the Philosophy Faculty, University of Zagreb. Since 2000, she collaborates with numerous organizations engaged in the field of cultural and artistic production as well as media in Croatia. From 2004 to 2009 she worked as PR, editor of publications, and executive producer for the Eurokaz – International Festival of New Theatre. As member of Kurziv – Platform for Matters of Culture, Media and Society, she was the publisher of the online publication Kulturpunkt.hr, from 2009 till 2018,

and has worked with media development, project management, and media and cultural policies. She was editor-in-chief of the portal Kulturpunkt.hr (2014–2018) and is in charge of two other programmes of the organization. She edited several publications and contributed to magazines specialized in culture and the performing arts, media, and education. Currently she works in the Department for Research and Development at Kultura Nova Foundation. She lives and works in Zagreb.

Nesrine Malik (b. 1990) is a British-Sudanese columnist and features writer for the *Guardian*. She was born in Sudan and grew up in Kenya, Egypt, and Saudi Arabia. She received her undergraduate education at the American University in Cairo and University of Khartoum, and her post graduate education at the University of London. Before her career as a journalist, she spent ten years in emerging markets private equity. She was named Society & Diversity Commentator of the Year at the 2017 Comment Awards.

Nadifa Mohamed (b. 1981, Hargeisa, Somalia) studied History and Politics at St. Hilda's College, Oxford University. Her first novel, *Black Mamba Boy*, won the Betty Trask Prize, was long-listed for the Orange Prize, and was short-listed for the Guardian First Book Award, and other prizes. In 2013 she was selected as one of Granta's Best of Young British Novelists and in 2014 as one of Africa 39's Best of Young African Novelists. Her second novel, *The Orchard of Lost Souls*, was published in 2013 and won a Somerset Maugham Prize and the Prix Albert Bernard, and was long-listed for The Dylan Thomas Prize and short-listed for the Hurston/Wright Legacy Award. Her work is translated into fourteen languages. She has just been announced as a 2018 recipient of an Arts and Literary Arts Fellowship from the Rockefeller Foundation and is a Fellow of the Royal Society of Literature.

Thomas Roueché (b.1986) is an editor, writer, and cultural consultant. He studied at the University of Cambridge and has an MA in Turkish Studies from the School of Oriental and African Studies, London. Roueché has completed editorial projects with the Prince Claus Fund, the European Cultural Foundation, and the Kurdistan Museum, including *Cultural Emergency Response in Conflict and Disaster* (2011) and *African Opera* (2017), amongst others. He is a contributing editor at *Cornucopia* magazine. Between 2014 and 2019 he was the editor of *TANK*, a magazine of contemporary culture based in London, where he is now on the editorial board. Roueché lives and works in London and Istanbul.

Ece Temelkuran (b.1973) is an author and a political commentator. She writes novels, poetry, and political non-fiction. Recent books include *How To Lose A Country: 7 Steps from Democracy to Dictatorship* (2019), *Women Who Blow on Knots* (2016), *The Time of Mute Swans* (2017), *Turkey: The Insane and the Melancholy* (2016). Temelkuran lives in Zagreb when she is not travelling.

Daniel Trilling (b.1981) is a journalist and editor of *New Humanist* magazine. He writes about migration, borders, and nationalism for several publications, including the *Guardian*, *London Review of Books* and *The New York Times*. Recent books include: *Lights in the Distance: Exile and Refuge at the Borders of Europe* (2018) and *Bloody Nasty People: The Rise of Britain's Far Right* (2012). Trilling lives and works in London.

Menno Weijs (b.1981) is project manager at the European Cultural Foundation. He was involved in several collaborative programmes and projects around media and the public sphere in Europe. Between 2016 and 2018 Menno was responsible for the strategic partnership 'Displaced in Media', aiming to develop an infrastructure that supports the inclusion of refugees and migrants in the public sphere. The European Cultural Foundation is an independent foundation based in Amsterdam that strives for an open, inclusive, and democratic Europe.

André Wilkens (b.1963) is the Director of the European Cultural Foundation in Amsterdam. He is also the Board Chair of Tactical Tech Cooperative, the co-founder of the Initiative Offene Gesellschaft, and a founding member of the European Council on Foreign Relations. In the past he worked as Director of the Mercator Centre Berlin, as Director of the Open Society Institute Brussels, and as Head of Strategic Communications of UNHCR in Geneva. His positions prior to this were at the Ogilvy & Mather communications agency in Brussels, the European Training Foundation in Turin and at the European Commission and European Parliament in Brussels. André is the author of two books on Europe and on digitalization, and a regular media contributor.

About the Contributors

IMAGE CREDITS

Roda Abdalle, *Avskild*, (*Decluded*),
2017, 3.00 min.
P. 141, 142, 149, 150

Anonymous, *Anonymous*,
2018, 4.06 min.
Courtesy of the artist
P. 83, 84, 93, 94

Tania Bruguera, *10,148,451*, Hyundai
Commission, Tate Modern, 2 October
2018–24 February 2019. © Tania Bruguera.
Photograph ©Tate, London, 2019.
Photograph: Benedict Johnson
P. 99, 110

Tania Bruguera, *10,148,451*, Hyundai
Commission, Tate Modern, 2 October
2018–24 February 2019. © Tania Bruguera.
Photograph © Tate, London, 2019
P. 100, 109

Banu Cennetoğlu, *The List*, 2018
Photo by Joe Anderson
P. 1, 168

Jillian Edelstein, *Life Seekers*, 2018,
photograph. Courtesy of the artist
P. 19, 20, 29, 30

Moha Gerehou, *The most racist
advertisements in history*, 2018, 5.19 min.
Courtesy of the artist
P. 35, 36, 43, 44

Mulham Mohamed Hidel, *It's not hard*,
2018, 5.41 min.
Courtesy of the artist
P. 49, 50, 57, 58

Lubaina Himid, *Negative Positives:
The Guardian Archive*, 2007–2017,
acrylic on newspaper.
Photos by Andy Keate.

Courtesy of the artist
and Hollybush Gardens
P. 127, 128, 135, 136

Jade Jackman, *Calling Home*,
2017, 3.36 min.
P. 115, 116, 121, 122

Jacob Lawrence, *The Migration Gained in
Momentum*, panel 18 from *The Migration
Series*, 1940–41. New York, Museum of
Modern Art. Casein tempera on hardboard,
18 × 12' (45.7 × 30.5 cm). Gift of Mrs. David
M. Levy. Acc. n.: 28.1942.9. © 2019.
Digital image, The Museum of Modern Art,
New York/Scala, Florence.
P. 63

Jacob Lawrence, *The Negro press
was also influential in urging the people
to leave the South*, panel 34 from
The Migration Series, 1940–41. New York,
Museum of Modern Art. Casein tempera
on hardboard, 18 × 12' (45.7 × 30.5 cm).
Gift of Mrs. David M. Levy. Acc. n.:
28.1942.17. © 2019. Digital image,
The Museum of Modern Art, New York/
Scala, Florence.
P. 64

Jacob Lawrence, *Race riots were
numerous. White workers were hostile
toward the migrants who had been
hired to break strikes*, panel 50 from
The Migration Series, 1940–41.
New York, Museum of Modern Art.
Tempera on gesso on composition board,
18 × 12' (45.7 × 30.5 cm). Gift of Mrs. David
M. Levy. Acc. n.: 28.1942.25. © 2019.
Digital image, The Museum of Modern Art,
New York/Scala, Florence.
P. 77

Jacob Lawrence, *One of the main forms of social and recreational activities in which the migrants indulged occurred in the church*, panel 54 from *The Migration Series*, 1940–41. New York, Museum of Modern Art. Casein tempera on hardboard, 12 × 18' (30.5 × 45.7 cm). Gift of Mrs. David M. Levy. Acc. n.: 28.1942.27. © 2019. Digital image, The Museum of Modern Art, New York/Scala, Florence.
P. 78

COLOPHON

Lost in Media
Migrant Perspectives
and the Public Sphere

Editors
Ismail Einashe, Thomas Roueché

Coordination
Susanne Mors, Menno Weijs

Contributors
Tania Bruguera
Moha Gerehou
Aleksandar Hemon
Lubaina Himid
Dawid Krawczyk
Antonija Letinić
Nesrine Malik
Nadifa Mohamed
Ece Temelkuran
Daniel Trilling
Menno Weijs
André Wilkens

Artistic Contributions
Anonymous
Roda Abdalle
Tania Bruguera
Jillian Edelstein
Moha Gerehou
Lubaina Himid
Jade Jackman
Jacob Lawrence
Mulham Mohamed Hidel

Copy Editing
Leo Reijnen

Proofreading
Els Brinkman

Graphic Design
Gerlinde Schuller, The World as Flatland

Paper
Lessebo Design Smooth

Lithography
Mariska Bijl, Wilco Art Books

Printing and Binding
Bariet Ten Brink, Meppel

Publisher
Pia Pol, Astrid Vorstermans /
Valiz, Amsterdam

Distribution
–BE/NL/LU: Centraal Boekhuis,
  www.centraal.boekhuis.nl
–GB/IE: Anagram Books,
  www.anagrambooks.com
–Europe/Asia: Idea Books,
  www.ideabooks.nl
–Australia: Perimeter Books,
  www.perimeterbooks.com
–USA: D.A.P., www.artbook.com
–Individual orders: www.valiz.nl;
  info@valiz.nl

For works of visual artists affiliated with
a CISAC-organization the copyrights
have been settled with Pictoright in
Amsterdam. © Pictoright, 2019

The editors and the publisher have made
every effort to secure permission to repro-
duce the listed material, texts, illustrations
and photographs. We apologize for any
inadvert errors or omissions. Parties
who nevertheless believe they can claim
specific legal rights are invited to contact
the publisher. info@valiz.nl

ISBN 978 94 92095 68 8

Printed and bound in the EU
Valiz, Amsterdam, 2019

valiz

Valiz is an independent international publisher on contemporary art, theory, critique, design and urban affairs.

Our books offer critical reflection, interdisciplinary inspiration, and often establish a connection between cultural disciplines and socio-political questions. We publish these books out of our commitment to their content, to artistic and social issues and to the artists, designers and authors.

Apart from publishing Valiz organizes lectures, debates and other cultural projects in which certain topics in contemporary art are explored.

www.valiz.nl

This publication was published in partnership with:
European Cultural Foundation, Amsterdam

European Cultural
Foundation

The European Cultural Foundation works for an open, inclusive and better Europe. It was created 65 years ago for the promotion of European unity by encouraging cultural and educational activities of common interest.

In 2019 the foundation's theme is 'Democracy Needs Imagination'. Because culture can provide resistance against divisive forces.

Culture can tell the story of Europe.
Culture can imagine a better future.

www.culturalfoundation.eu

Colophon

List of 34,361 documented deaths of refugees and migrants due to the restrictive policies of "Fortress Europe"
S NOT REFUGEES!